Story of a Marriage

Copyright © 2024 by James McCormick
All world rights reserved.

No part of this book may be reproduced, stored in a retrieval system, or transmitted in any form or by any means electronic, mechanical, photocopying, recording or otherwise, without the prior consent of the publisher.

Readers are encouraged to go to MissionPointPress.com to contact the author or to find information on how to buy this book in bulk at a discounted rate.

MISSION POINT PRESS

Published by Mission Point Press
2554 Chandler Rd.
Traverse City, MI 49696
(231) 421-9513
MissionPointPress.com

Softcover: 978-1-961302-83-9
Hardcover: 978-1-961302-84-6

Library of Congress Control Number: 2024914645

Printed in the United States of America

Story of a Marriage

50 YEARS OF CHRISTMAS LOVE LETTERS

JIM McCORMICK

MISSION POINT PRESS

May the rhythms of daily life
Give new strength to your love and faith.
May you triumph over foolish strife
And come home together sound and safe.

May troubles give you in their turn
A challenge to begin again.
May you with hope and joy thus learn
Surely that love need never end.

From "A Wedding Blessing," by Andrew Greeley, 1991

Contents

Preface ... ix

Explanatory Note to the Reader ... xi

The Early Years 1968–1976 ... 1

Raising a Family 1977–1994 ... 21

Photo Addendum ... 57

Middle Age Marriage 1995–2000 ... 71

Early Retirement 2001–2010 ... 87

Later Life, and Death, of a Partner 2011–2018 ... 105

Epilogue #1—2020 ... 123

Epilogue #2—2023 ... 125

About the Author ... 127

Preface

When Marilyn was close to death in October 2018, I asked her where she had hidden all the Christmas love letters I had written to her since our first Christmas in 1968, fifty years earlier. She said, in a weak voice, that they were on a high shelf in her bedroom.

I panicked when I couldn't find them. I knew they told the story of our lives together, at least from my perspective. Were they lost forever? Thank God our son David, in a more thorough search, found them all.

The sweet, the critical, the apologetic, the poetic. The newlyweds, the child-centered years, strains on our love, time for world travel, growing old together. All our linen "hung out."

Should we share our married life with the world? Could I speak for her in that regard? Did we have something important to say to a world in which lifelong successful marriages are hard to achieve?

I have decided the answer is "yes." I hope that by following our steps from the period of young marriage to the struggle with personality conflicts to the dug-in commitment of mature marriage, the reader will find something authentic, real, helpful. Ours was not a "marriage made in heaven." If we made it together for fifty years, maybe you can too!

The "book" started by accident. I wrote a love letter to Marilyn on Christmas Eve, 1968, our first Christmas together. Lo and behold, she loved it so much she begged me to write a Christmas letter to her every year as long as we lived. I said I would, of course, but I had no idea where that would lead. Fifty years of our lives spread out on paper, one year at a time. Almost no one writes like that anymore.

I have not found many recent parallels to this writing longevity, but one truly inspires me. That is *The Prison Letters of Nelson Mandela*, written by this great man during the twenty-seven years of imprisonment, mostly at the notorious Robben Island Prison in South Africa. A real Christ figure, he never lost his humanity, his compassion, his forgiveness.

Two months after my dear wife's passing, I penned my last Christmas letter to her. By far my most passionate love letter. Grief-stricken, despairing, filled with a depth of love I had never before felt or expressed. Painful, but beautiful. It is how I still feel today.

Five years later I am finally able to share this story. My memories are mostly happy ones now. This book is my tribute to Marilyn. A poor man's Taj Mahal.

Explanatory Note to the Reader

As these are letters to my wife, some facts and names are taken for granted. For example, I didn't have to tell her we had difficulty getting pregnant! So, a brief summary of our "journey" may help you comprehend what otherwise may appear puzzling.

We were married in April 1968. She was 26 and I was 33. After one year we moved "up north" from Detroit to the beautiful tourist town of Traverse City. In 1970 I was badly burned while on a hunting trip and spent two months in the local hospital, leaving her home alone with our infant, newly adopted son Danny. I worked as a lawyer, she as a high school English and religion teacher at St. Francis High School. Two years later we adopted a second baby, Ginny. In 1976 a third baby, David, was born to us, a big surprise.

Later that year, I was elected to a local judgeship, where I served 24 years. In 1979 son Danny was diagnosed with a tumor on his pituitary gland, which altered our family life. He recovered from brain surgery but was plagued with health problems all his life. It took a toll on all of us and will help to explain some of our marital stresses.

Our daughter, Ginny, is married to Darric Newman. They have two wonderful sons, Cameron and Ben, with whom I am very close in my old age.

The 2006 letter, in poetry and song, was addressed to our son David's marriage in Seoul to his Korean bride, Lee Ji-eun.

I speak of the typical marital conflicts which affect most healthy marriages, but perhaps I should underline the difficulties which come with depression. Marilyn would say she experienced some degree of anxiety and depression, periodically, from high school on. Her therapist referred to it as cyclothymia. This includes periods of high energy, and creativity, sometimes followed by periods of feeling sad. These mood swings are relatively mild, but the downness caused much angst. They present a challenge in a marriage, as you will see.

Despite this, we had a great marriage. Marilyn would agree.

A few of the letters were not found with the rest. I would guess she misplaced them. I have filled in those gaps with a few romantic notes written over the years by her to me and by me to her.

I still have my original, longhand letters, thanks to Marilyn keeping them in a box, hidden on a shelf. I have included the first one, on our New Orleans hotel stationery. (See cover.) I think it conveys an intimacy which a keyboard cannot. Picture all the letters in the original form.

The Early Years
1968–1976

~~~~~~

CHRISTMAS 1968

First Christmas

Dear Darling Lyn,
May this be the merriest Christmas of your young beautiful life and may each succeeding one be brighter and more satisfying by virtue of your growth as a warm, loving woman.

This Christmas letter is quite ironic, since one of the great accomplishments of the last 12 months for me has been learning how to enter your heart and how to open up my crusty old heart to the kind of deep, compromising relationship which we have been building, one pout, "crisis," freeze, thaw, smile, quip, squeeze of the hand, ecstatic reconciliation, contented glow at a time. Ironic, I say, because I have no real need to place my innermost feelings about you in writing in order to avoid the embarrassment of speaking them to your face. I love to say these things to you, person to person, because somehow you have forced me to enter into the daylight and learn to share my life with someone other than myself.

While I could readily say all of this in the comfortable privacy of our room, I want you to have it in writing for the occasional rough days when you may need a reminder of my love for you. As you well know, I find it hard to talk when I get in one of those grouchy moods. Yet even then I am restless for the return of my sanity so that I can squeeze the breath out of you and make you happy again.

I hope you like the Monteleone stationery. I have been looking for it for a week, because it seemed so fitting. Those were glorious, exciting, tremulous days. We couldn't believe we could suddenly be so happy, so mutually satisfied, so ready for our common future. There we were, as green about marriage as one can be, uncertain about our technical proficiency at the art of love … but so happy with each other and so concerned about each other's feelings.

We learned a big lesson in New Orleans, honey, and, as you well recall, the lesson is that we learn and grow and benefit from having to wait and worry, and that we appreciate what we get after having been denied it when we first sought it. Now we are back in New Orleans staying at the Monteleone again. This time we are a little anxious about getting a wee one started. Let us find the courage and hope we discovered in New Orleans once before, and let us forever be conscious that our devotion does not depend upon external circumstances of fortune but upon our love and respect for each other. You are my concrete rock in the face of change and an unpredictable future which may raise us on high or lay us low. If we keep this one certainty—our security in each other's love—we have nothing to ever fear. And we will find many ways to pass on to others the overflow from our union of love. That, I guess, is the test of the authenticity of our relationship.

So far it looks like a success.

Your grateful husband,

Jim

CHRISTMAS 1969

We move up North

Dear Sweetie Pie,

You said that traditions are important in a family, so I finally got around to keeping this one alive. Merry Christmas and the best there is in 1970, honey.

I started gathering ideas for my annual Christmas letter in early December, but I just couldn't locate any of our stationery from romantic stops along the way, like Atitlan or Macuto or San Jose, Costa Rica, or the Monteleone Hotel. Not even an envelope from the blue Caribbean in Barbados, or the friendly roadside cabins in the copper country, across from Jacobs Ladder.

Then a brilliant idea for a coup of the heart struck me— why not go through the tunnel to Windsor and go to the check-in desk at the Holiday Inn—where we went after the wedding feast—and ask for some of the stationery. Jerry Sihle and I did just that, but I proceeded to misplace it, at which point I lost heart. Then, lo and behold, Stu and John came through and saved the tradition by coming up with our new law firm stationery.

I knew you'd be proud of it since you're kind of partial to me. I have to candidly admit that it looks awfully good to me. I guess it symbolizes our big adventure in pulling up stakes and moving north. If you recall, Traverse City was a remote dream when I wrote to you last Christmas. Already it is becoming home.

To say that the adventure of the last year could not have happened to me without you would be a gross understatement. You are such a loyal friend. There were days and weeks last summer when you were the only thing I had to hold onto, and you were a bastion of strength. You still are, every day in so many ways.

You might get the impression, honey, that coming to T.C. is the only adventure I took part in this last year. That is far from the truth. Just getting to know you better, relaxing in your fond presence, enjoying your company … has been the true adventure of 1969 for me.

Watching you captivate the students and faculty at St. Francis High with your dynamite personality has been a pleasure too. It's good to see others enjoying what I am privileged to enjoy every day of my life.

Well, sweetheart, the year ended with your giving me a priceless little puppy. Phineas has to symbolize the family which is coming next.

When the kids start to arrive life is going to change around here. Knowing you, I'm confident it will be a real adventure, which will last well past our lives. Next Christmas I'll be able to get a little more specific, okay?

It's been a wonderful year, little one, and here's to about 60 more, even better and more mellow as time goes on.

Turning inside and out with love for you,
Jim

CHRISTMAS 1970

Our first baby

What a switch from last year, when we were just coming into our own in Traverse City but nevertheless still feeling that Detroit was home! Now we feel secure here, among good friends, with a future we needn't fear. But then the lesson from this is that we should never look forward with fear, because we make our own futures, with the ever-present guidance of the Lord.

This year, 1970, has brought me confidence in practicing law in northern Michigan, has brought us a million blessings in Danny, and has presented us both with numerous opportunities for development of ourselves as people who give rather than take. We have handled some of those opportunities well. There was the Adult Ed. Group, with the pressure on you to organize things. And, of course, the month culminating in the graduation of your senior class from St. Francis High. You were so wrapped up in the welfare of those kids. Your ability to share yourself with so many of them never ceased to amaze and please me. They still come to see you for inspiration and advice—I think you symbolize continuity with their past and spunk in meeting their individual futures.

I should not end this letter without reference to your sometimes traumatic meetings of the penta-council, as you metamorphosed from parliamentary advisor to female gadfly. All good clean fun, and, who knows, maybe even productive of results some day. FISH, on the other hand, was your tour de force. Results, in the form of help to people in need, were produced in record time—and you were a very important part of it. Makes a husband mighty proud.

I love to see you absorbed in such things, honey, because admiring you is part of loving you. With our little Danny around there is less time for such things now, but then there is the realization that we, particularly you, are creating the environment which will help him to grow up to be the finest man around. Danny and the little brother and sisters we hope to give him will help to move the human race a small step closer to that omega point of perfect humanity. In other words, our hopes for that little boy, while unstructured, are high. If, during 1970, we have started him on the path to a happy, basically unselfish life, then it has been a successful year for us.

We will have many heartaches this next year, darling, as in every year. Most will evaporate, as did our concern over not having "our own" children born to us. As in this instance, if we are true to our commitment to love others as much as we love ourselves, we will always find answers. Danny is a beautiful answer. He is also, and much more importantly, a little person for us to love and care for in a very intimate way. Even if he weren't such a magnificent little boy this would still be true. He is ours to love and enjoy.

Sweetheart—how did we get through the summer of 1970? What with our excitement over Daniel Francis McCormick, my sometimes tense migrant farm workers meetings, and Jerry - Linda - Carlene and all the migrant camp situations they involved us in? It was a positive, exciting summer. As much as I suffered over some of my law student migrant interactions, it was a period of growth for me. I got more satisfaction from those weeks helping the migrants than from a hundred business clients. I am afraid it has turned me farther towards the idea of serving the poor. I am confident the Spirit is at work. I don't like to be jogged out of my comfort zone any more than you do, and any further moves in that direction will take a joint resolve on our part. I know the opportunity will present itself, and life is too short to let yourself live it in a business-as-usual fashion. I dearly love the Hubbell law firm and I hope we can stay with them professionally while still providing me with an outlet for this need to serve. But giving up nice things brings temporary distress, and we may have to face that some day. Our real gladness has to be with ourselves. (I think I have myself convinced, for the moment.)

We have lived another whole year together since I last wrote to you. That should mean more understanding and tolerance for each other's faults. I think it has. That should mean an increase in the trust we place in each other. I think it has. That should mean greater comfort in each other when things go all wrong. I know it has.

These last six weeks, in the hospital with burns from my hunting accident, have taught me something about our dependence on others. At times I have sucked you dry in satisfaction of my need for consolation. So many other people have communicated their grief to me and assured me they were "with me" in my suffering. Their words have helped, in varying degrees, to assuage the feeling of hopelessness and isolation which accompanies such pain when it goes on for a long time. Still I have come back to you for my primary solace. I have wanted you to <u>understand</u> the agony and anxiety. I have needed complete rapport with you, a full sharing of the experience on the level of understanding and caring. This is because I can't bear to carry the burden alone. If I didn't have you it would be different. I would have no choice except to suffer within myself. But I do have you, thank God, and I have been able to pour out my anguish on your lovely shoulders. I really don't know how my pain has affected you, having never been in your position. At times the burden has been too much for either of us to carry. That has not been for long at a time. I do know it has been very hard on you, which simply means that you do identify with me to a great degree.

Sweetheart, this hunting accident has shaken me to the quick. It has upset our lives. It has strained our relationship. It has shown who our friends are. It has produced an outpouring of kindness and feeling from a great number of people. I hope it will somehow make me a better person. If not, it will seem to me to have been a cruel waste. As it is, I think we will see our mutual feelings grow stronger and our love more sensitive to each other's needs.

We will step into 1971 with faith in God and in one another strengthened. There is nothing to fear. It's going to be great fun loving you and Danny. Here we go—all together.

Merry Xmas Sweety Pie.

Love,

Jim

Story of a Marriage

CHRISTMAS 1971

Our life in poetry

By the time we got to Windsor
I was worried, would we be the lovers
we had waited for.
And by morning we were closer
but a distance still apart.
So I trembled as we rode to Metro to depart.
By the time we reached New Orleans
I was thumbing every last erotic handbook
on the shelf, and we feasted on the city and returned
to our own room. To a love which raged like fire
but would not consume.
By the time we left Guatemala I was bursting like
a savage who had slain the dinosaur.
Like a youth who had at last felt full
of lovely women's flesh.
Like a man who'd need his wife's dear body
from that hour.
By the time we found Traverse City we were lovers.
Oh I think we meet the test in every way.
Soul and body I am yours to handle gently or destroy.
And I'll travel on forever with you if I may.

Happy 1972 Sweety Pie,
Love, Jim

Jim McCormick

CHRISTMAS 1972

Getting ready for a second baby

Dear Marilyn,

Let's have a very Merry Christmas together again! Thank you for making my life worthwhile for another year.

You know, honey, I'm not very inspired tonight, so don't get your crying towel out. No original song, no reviews of tumultuous days, no very touching phrases. The muse is not available at the moment, but the feeling is surely alive.

To put it succinctly, if prosaically, my love for you grows as we live together longer and as I learn more about life.

The picture on the stationery represents a fantasy but it's one I like and associate with you. I hope you don't mind the "erotic" nature of the drawing. I didn't think you'd mind. After all, it's only us, little sweety pie. You have grown a lot in the last five years, and that has made you a lot more lovable too. That partly explains my feelings about you. We were both younger but less human when we met. Now my trust in you is close to absolute. I know your feelings have followed a similar progression.

Well, we need all the family strength at our command now, since we are about to enlarge that little family by one. Thank the Lord we are going forward with a clear idea of who we are and where we are headed. The little one will most certainly benefit from what we have learned this year about life and death and the good Lord who watches over us every day. May he take special care of the four of us this year.

I happened to read something today taken from Peter Marshall's writings. It struck me as a good prayer for us to think about and try to recall in the big day ahead. So as not to lose it, I'll assure its immortality for all at least a few years by including it here:

"Lord, help us to stand for what is right, not because it may yield dividends later, but because it is right now. Help us to know no barriers of creed or race, that our love may be like thine—a love that sees all men as thy children and our brothers. Amen."

Well, honey, even though this has been heavy on the philosophical, it is written on the paper I chose to remind you that my love for you is as physical as it is spiritual. The two are well-mixed up by now, as it should be. To you (& Danny) good night and good year.

Love, Jim

Birthday Message 1973

Jim darling,

You are truly a wonderful partner for the kids and "I bless the day you were born." That saying reminds me of two others: "Somewhere in my youth and childhood I must have done something good." and "I knew you before you were born and called you by name." What I mean is I feel we are part of God's plan for each other's souls and your birthday is an important day in that plan.

   I love you very much.

   Marilyn

~~~~~~~~~~

(I guess she lost my Christmas letter for 1973, so I found a note she wrote to me that year.)

CHRISTMAS 1974

An exchange student enriches our lives

Merry Christmas again, Honey,
A tradition like this should never be allowed to die, even in busy years. After all, it will be a good record of our comings and goings when we get these letters out in 1985 or 1995 or 2005 or even 2015. By then the letterheads from New Orleans, Windsor, maybe even Traverse City, will seem quaint reminders of our frantic early years.

By 1974 our marriage has become part of us, to the extent that it's hard to remember being a "single" loner. We don't reflect very often on what we have built together, but it is something beautiful. I know you and you know me. We share a common philosophy of life and an outlook on other people. Marriage can be too exclusive an arrangement, even smug. Ours isn't. We have included many, many people in our good fortune. You have made this possible. I feel I'm the theoretician but you execute the plan.

This last year we added Gabriel Ibrahim Gutierrez, A.K.A. "Biel," to our world. Because Biel is from another world we will not see much of him in the future, but he will always be part of us and we will be part of his life. That much we know. When he arrived in Traverse City last January we immediately knew our Brazilian "son" would add a dimension to our lives. He did even more than that. He taught us something about life. He affected Danny's life too, and for that we will ever thank him. We may never again become so intimate with a "foreigner." He showed us that human sensitivity and humor and character occur everywhere on the globe. God bless him and the family which bore and raised him.

This has also been the year in which Mary Virginia McCormick came into her own with a vengeance. By now she has earned herself a permanent and unique place in my heart. You saw Ginny's special little personality much earlier than I did, I confess. For me she blossomed into a very delightful little girl last summer, after a difficult first two years. I always loved her because she was ours, but now I look forward to seeing her because I know she will say something cute and will demonstrate her special spunk, independence, and intelligence. What a little pixie she has become.

By now Danny has found most of his presents and is humoring us about Santa Claus bringing them tonight. He's too smart and sweet and irresistible. But one of these days he'll be a juvenile and we will look back with a sigh on the beautiful period of his little boyhood. Let's capture more of it for the future. Tapes would help. Our memories otherwise might fail us someday and we would no longer be able to relive Danny at 4 ½ years old.

In 1975 we are going to Brazil to visit the boy wonder and to have another great adventure together. I have it all planned in my head. I assure you it will be great. No dugout canoes this time, but there will be some experiences to savor for a lifetime.

A lifetime, indeed. I pray to the Father that it will be spent together, that nothing will ever separate us until we both have lived out our full times on the earth. Then we can regroup in the life prepared for us forever. Death is not the only force that can alter that plan. There is also the possibility, especially today, of growing apart through indifference, selfishness and lack of effort. I hereby pledge my best to honor and love you forever, to bury my self-centered preference for having everything my way, to stifle my penchant for criticism of anything that doesn't exactly suit my preferences. I can be a harsh judge at home, wanting you to remake your already beautiful self to harmonize precisely with my notions of how one should talk, laugh, think. Fortunately, your ego is healthy. You know where I get my critical habits. At the communal confession last week I put this problem of mine in God's hands. It is my problem, not yours. I would be critical of little things about anyone as close to me as you are.

Anyway, I love and respect you for yourself, your ideas, your heart, your pretty face, your good family, your loving nature. What more can I say?

That's 1974. Here's to 1975 and many more years of striving together. May our harmony grow at home and our accomplishments grow outside the home.

Your husband and partner in life,
Jim

Love Letter 1975

Dearest Jim,

This has been a wonderful retreat. I told you lots of small stuff on the phone. Thanks for being there when I got home. I would not like life very much without my "partner."

You make so many things possible for me! I told you, you are a gentle man. I love you very much!

This sleeping alone is for the birds. I hope they like it. I don't!

Love,
Marilyn

~~~~~~~~~~~~~~~~

(I guess she lost my 1975 Christmas letter too, so the above note found, dated in 1975, will show we were still together.)

Valentine's Day 1976

Dear Marilyn,
Unlike you, I don't know exactly how I would be without you. It's because I never allow myself to reflect on such catastrophic possibilities. Long ago you became as much a part of me as my conscience.
  Your male half,
  Jim McCormick

(I came across this in Marilyn's dresser drawer, after she died. It looks like a reply to her 1975 love note to me.)

Jim McCormick

CHRISTMAS 1976

A baby son and a wonderful year

Dear Marilyn,
1976 has been a wonderful year for all of us: You delivered our little Davey in January; Danny started at St. Francis school. Ginny became a little lady instead of a toddler. Davey grew strong and healthy, and I realized a great dream—election to the District Court. Ron was ordained a priest. And Mike and Karen committed themselves to each other for life and eternity. Which makes me reflect on our commitment to love, honor and cherish forever. We have our share of arguments and faults, honey, but I think we have done a good job of keeping in mind the reason we married one another and the permanency of our life together. With Divine blessing you and I will be together until a ripe and satisfying old age. Then we will await the day of reunion in the next life. So, get used to me; I'll be part of you long after we both part from this sojourn on this chosen planet. The details of the future may be, and are uncertain, but the essence of it is in our hands. If we love and shelter one another, through thick and thin, we are doing God's will and will grow ever closer to each other.

Honey, I am not very good about expressing my feelings for you, because I take your love of me for granted and assume you instantly know how I feel. You are first of all, a perfect friend. Always interesting, stimulating, full of ideas for things to do, worrying about me, anticipating my needs, confiding your own thoughts and cares. Loyalty is your middle name. And that is a characteristic of love. You are also very sensitive to my moods and are everything I could want in terms of our physical union.

Some things about a lover are subjective. For example, I just happen to like your looks, the shape of your face, your jaw, your pretty, gentle eyes, your sensuous and perfectly shaped mouth, your neck, your body … I love you for everything you do for our kids. You, above all, are molding the direction of their lives, and they are responding. Their health, vitality, enthusiasm for life, inquisitiveness, and warmth are all testimonials to the love you have given them.

I love you for everything you have done for me as a person. I know I am a much better man and much happier one than I would have been without <u>you</u>.

So I promise to love, honor and cherish you, Marilyn Frances Torina McCormick, until the end of time, as long as love Himself lasts.

With meaning,

Jim

Raising a Family
1977–1994

CHRISTMAS 1977

A slightly tempestuous relationship

Dear Marilyn,

I don't feel very inspired by the muse today. But it is almost Christmas so I will write down what comes to mind. I think a little adversity makes us more creative, and this has been a year of peace and prosperity, fulfillment and contentment, for me at least. For a number of years you wondered whether I would still be flying all over Michigan in another ten or twenty years. I didn't know, and, although I wasn't worrying too much about what the future would bring, I didn't like the thought of dragging my old body off to catch pre-dawn planes at the age of sixty or sixty-five, at least not on a regular basis. If there is a moral to this it is that we must concentrate upon living in the present to the fullest and leaving tomorrow in the hands of the providential Father.

One of the reasons I maintain this Xmas letter tradition is that it provides a wonderful opportunity to sermonize and moralize. End of sermon!

It also gives me the chance to tell you, on the record, how much I love you and how grateful I am to have found you. I instinctively knew when I met "Lyn Torina," that I was going to be pulled to her with a magnetic effect. We are very different temperamentally, which makes for a slightly tempestuous relationship, but the pluses of knowing you intimately and sharing your heart far outweigh the little disruptions we have from time to time.

If you were but wise and good, but not much fun, it would suffice for me. If you were wise and good and fun, but not so loving, it would suffice for me. If you were but wise and good and fun and loving, but not so beautiful, it would suffice for me. If you were wise, good, fun, loving & beautiful, but not someone with whom I can share each little detail of my day and each little twist of the law, it would suffice for me.

But you are all of these things. You were made to make me happy and fulfilled. I hope I can do the same for you.

Love,
Jim

Jim McCormick

Love Letter 1977

Dearest Jim,
You probably think this is another note about the kids or house but it isn't. It is, I guess, a love letter. I didn't realize until I began to write this, how shy and embarrassed I would feel. (I think I am so free.)

I spent this morning feeling very nervous about leaving you for a few days. Not about the house and kids, but you. You are such a part of me. Who will I share my thoughts and feelings with? Who will make me feel safe in bed? Who will my existence reflect? I love you very much, Jim. You are the dearest, strongest, kindest, most fun person I have ever known. You are the part of me that is missing. Maybe that is what scripture really means when it says, "the two shall be as one." I am really not complete without you. You are strong when I am weak, steady when I am frantic, light when I am heavy, fun when I am too sober. I love your integrity, your very fine mind, your very attractive body.

I am very blessed to have a husband that is everything I ever desired in a man.

We are very lucky, my love. Don't ever let us forget it.
All my love,
Marilyn

CHRISTMAS 1978

Not so much intimacy

Dear Marilyn,
As I start to write this letter you are in the kitchen involved in a very long telephone conversation with your family. The kids are in bed. They will be up in eight hours. There must be thirty packages under the tree; with many more to arrive in a couple days when your folks come up from Detroit. The stockings are stuffed and hanging by the fireplace where they belong. The snow is just deep enough to set the proper atmosphere for Christmas. So far we have had two gatherings here during the season. The first was the cocktail party before my office party. You did a beautiful job of entertaining everyone. It looks as if the kids will get far too many things this year as always. We are getting each other small things since we are broke. Maybe this is just as well since we live in the most consumption-minded culture of all times. Next year we'll probably have our budget balanced and will spend a lot. We won't be any happier for it.

I've been setting some things down in this letter so that memories will be stirred in years to come if we should ever reread the letters. It's also a way to warm up to talking about us, you know, the two people who merged our separate futures on 4-15-68 at that classy church in the farms. Where have we come since then? Has it been worth the effort? Were we right for each other? Is Maue's cynical judgment on marriage right on the money? Is it just a truce, or a partnership in which we each figure we get enough to keep up the investment? Have we actually grown together that much? Or is it just a mutual accommodation, a detente which is mutually satisfactory? Do you really care about me, or do you just care that I am around to fill out the nuclear family role I am expected to play? You recently said, "I don't understand you at all," and I agree with that. But I think you are equally superficial in your understanding of me and how I feel.

So why did we quit the Marriage Encounter love letters so quickly? I guess we decided it was a big bore, or just plain unnecessary. The daily thing was too much, but we should have kept it up at least on a weekly basis. I'd like to start again, this week. Tonight I feel fairly unloved, despite monumental Christmas preparations all around me. I know you have worked and worried a great deal over that office party, and I appreciate that very much. I also am delighted that you put so much effort into making Christmas memorable and fun and holy for Dan, Ginny and Davey. But there hasn't been much contact between you and me recently and what there has been hasn't been that good. I don't mean just sex, I mean intimacy. I take my share of responsibility for all of that. I haven't been going out of my way to be loving, just doing my job.

What a time to be writing a Christmas letter to my wife! Maybe it's just the mood and the hour. It's been a great year in some ways. For example, our trip out west to Reno and California was a great experience and one we enjoyed together all the way. We have seen the three kids grow bigger, brighter, cuter and more interesting month by month. I love judging and don't care if I ever do anything else for the rest of my life. What more can I ask for? Really, nothing much. My feeling about "us" right now is more a case of a temporary lull than a cooling off of love in the sense of commitment to another person. I am more committed to you than ever. I just don't like this "old married couple" settling down routine. You are more beautiful to me now than you have ever been, so there is no reason for my interest in you as a person-lover to die down. We just need to pay more attention to one another's emotional needs. That's where those marriage encounter techniques come in handy.

I can't wait to get back on a more intimate, loving, feeling level with you again, honey, let's let it begin today, lover.

Merry Christmas,
Jim

Jim McCormick

CHRISTMAS 1979

Partners 'til the end

Dear Marilyn,
The twelfth year of our Christmas, 1979
Have you ever tried to pen a poem
when you're not inspired?
To tell your wife how sweet she is
when you're not so fired?
To gather your thoughts 'bout life and love
in a restaurant booth?
Mid clamor of shoppers' laughter,
din and talk uncouth?
Well it doesn't take a lot of reflection
about the human condition,
Compiling of lists of merits or acts of contrition
To compose a simple line of verse about my lady fair!
Her warmth, her spontaneity
comfort you everywhere.
They call her Lyn or Marilyn.
She sometimes calls me Mac.
I like it when she says that word.
It means we're on the track.
We fight, we laugh, we disagree,
we're partners 'til the end.
In friendship I'd ere yet be rich
were she my only friend.

Jamie McCormick

12-25-79

CHRISTMAS 1981

Dependent am I now upon your style

Dearest Marilyn,
Your mom and dad left for Detroit today. Soon we will all be back to our workaday lives, beginning 1982, hopefully as good a year as 1981, or 1968!

> [Remember Santiago Atitlan?
> You cried, but then such ecstasy my hon.
> Discovery of a manhood I'd suppressed—
> Like Tarzan mating Jane I beat my chest.]

The fire's burning bright in the family room, radiating warmth and reflecting color throughout the room. It's 15 degrees outside at 10:30 PM. At least a foot of fresh fluffy white stuff lies on the ground. Makes you want to crawl in bed with the girl you live with and become as one, probably wearing nothing but an electric blanket.

> [From Atitlan to Northern Michigan,
> From Guatemala's poor to Leelanau County.
> From the nervous pace of Detroit to this,
> Our harbor snug, with kith and kin our bounty.]

This year alone has had its share of family adventure and shared experiences. The highlight had to be our family trip to Northern Ontario. We sure handled camper living a lot better than the year before. The leisurely stay on Manitoulin Island, our pilgrimage to the Martyrs' shrine on Georgian Bay (watching Danny pray for a special healing), the weird deja vu of entering the Hospital for Sick

Children, the thrill of ethnic Toronto, the pleasant surprise that was Niagara-on-the-Lake.

And let's not soon forget our idyll in Petoskey last spring (where I got this stationery in contemplation of this letter). A very intimate few days it was for you and me.

It's been hard watching you suffer through the fall at St. Francis High. I realized how frustrated, angry and hurt you were at times. The students were so poorly mannered and undisciplined. Perhaps times have changed. Maybe it was the subject matter and the age group. I do know I've felt helpless watching you in such a trying situation. Now things seem to be getting manageable, thank the Lord. May he bless your efforts. You have something very special to give to those kids.

Poland and El Salvador happened this year too ... great tragedies on the world stage. What a year for us all!

The kids, our common endeavor, have been developing nicely, coming into their own as individuals with special talents and personalities. How pleased I am with each of them in their own ways. And what of "us"? Is our affair growing with the years, just drifting along, or weakening from neglect? Let me tell you why I feel positive about us, at least from my perspective:

> My thoughts, my friends, my life I owe to you.
> You've weaved a web about our lives, it's true.
> Instinctively, much like a poet rhymes,
> As if you'd made a home a thousand times.
> Dependent am I now upon your style,
> Don't want to face the future single file.
> The muse did make Kahlil Gibran a liar,
> _Inter_dependency is love's true fire.

Marilyn, I am grateful to you for your loyalty, sometimes blind loyalty, which is a real test of friendship. And I admire your concern for people around us, your ability to feel outrage about injustices, your finding time for people like Florence, your kindness to my mom and dad and family, your dedication to Dan, Ginny & Davey, your being a good listener for your many friends. All these things have matured in you over the past fourteen years since we decided to pool our futures. You have come to be so aware of my mood and emotional needs.

I deeply feel you have fashioned us into a family with roots, traditions, continuity. You have created a "myth" for the five of us. And you give me love and self-esteem. And, yes, I always enjoy your presence, conversing with you about almost anything (except furniture), doing things and going places with you, more so than with anyone else in the world. I guess that means I love you very much.

I guess I could, if I ever had to, adjust to life without you. In the meantime, I'll lock the doors, check the lights, let the dog out, dial down the thermostat, come upstairs and crawl in bed with my cuddly little kitten. I'll be right up!

All my love,
Jim

Jim McCormick

CHRISTMAS 1983

I'm very proud of you

Dear Marilyn, alias Honey, A.K.A. Sweetheart:
May this be one of your merriest Christmas seasons ever! I'm writing this early, on Friday December 9th, in my office at the courthouse, between hearings. Not very romantic surroundings, but it's quiet right now and I'm in a sentimental mood.

Other people seem to be attracting lightning lately. But not us. Marian Cram's illness may be bad, Grandma Norris just dropped dead. Many people in town are looking for work unsuccessfully. It's a time of grief. Maybe that's always the case. It just depends who is getting the brunt of it at the moment.

We aren't, thank the good God whose providence governs the world. Despite the usual friction created by parent-children tensions as well as in-fighting among the kids, all five of us are on a pretty even keel. Your teaching has been a huge success this year; a whole new challenge met with distinction. You ought to be extremely pleased with your accomplishments for the Catholic schools in the area of academic enrichment for all the kids, including the gifted and talented. I'm very proud of you. For this as well as for your everyday contribution to the well-being of so many people, especially your friends.

Dan, AKA Danny, Danny Boy, Franiel, Mack, etc. continues to thrive in school and in sports despite his glandular deficiency. His trauma over the growth shots has been a challenge for me lately but I'm very happy I have found some people in Munson Hospital who care and will meet with Dan and me to work it out.

Ginny is blooming as our straight "A" student this year. She's maturing fast and needs so much affection from us. Our father-daughter relationship is in high gear.

Davey is his own man, independent and bright and so "laid back." I talked to Annette Plamondon while I was on playground duty today. She said David is the only student in her class who is unaffected by her behavior modification system of rewards for good behavior. She surmises he's too smart and self-sufficient to need the rewards she has to offer. I hope that's the explanation. The kids at school all volunteered that Davey is very bad in class, always talking. Let's hope it stops at that. Annette didn't seem concerned about David as such, only about her difficulty in maintaining order in class.

Anyway, when you stand back and consider things with a bit of perspective it's obvious that these are some of the best years of our lives. Our children are becoming more involved in activities, making our days and nights busy and rich. Never a dull moment could be our lament. Elderly people envy these years. Couples just starting a family envy us too, as do single people and lonely people. When was the last time you were lonely? As for me, I can't remember.

As I conclude my seventh year as a judge I am still grateful for the rare opportunity to serve in this capacity. It's such a privilege as I see it. Not that there aren't tedious or stressful times, but overall it's my dream come true.

So are you, despite my critical nature. We have jelled as a good team. I am fulfilled in every way by you. I lack nothing I need, financially, socially, emotionally ... mainly thanks to you. When you feel good about yourself and your life, as I do, you are liberated to start considering other people. I feel that way, again to a large extent because of you.

In addition to being a loving woman with a big heart and a mind to match, you are even beautiful to look at. From a sheer aesthetic point of view, every feature of your face pleases my eyes: Your eyes, nose, mouth, forehead, cheekbones, chin, hair. I always was attracted to bright women with pretty faces. Imagine my luck in marrying one.

We must not let the little irritations of daily life blind us to our overall good fortune. The good Lord has blessed us generously. Thank you for being my biggest blessing.

All my love,

Jim

CHRISTMAS 1984

Merry Christmas Wife,
You are many things to many people, but I'm the lucky one who claims you for that intimate lifelong companionship. To the kids—Dan, Ginny & Davey—you are Mother, but they won't be there every day when you're old and gray. Your family—your mom & dad, sisters and brothers, aunts and uncles—share your blood and your memories of childhood and youth, but each has someone else to turn to in times of trouble or happiness. I have <u>you</u>.

Your host of friends give spice to your life and bring out the best in you as a person. But each has her own little universe. <u>I</u> am spinning around as the nucleus of yours. Proton and electron we may be, as different as possible to imagine, but just let anyone try to split our little atom! We are in this for good, forever. Until death does admit us to a better sphere, where God no doubt will continue our interdependence as perfect love, finally.

So why do I take you for granted most of the time? I guess it's my selfish nature. Maybe I can raise my consciousness of the beautiful gem I have found. I am going to try. And if sitting down to write this Christmas letter moves me in that direction it will have been time well spent. You deserve the best I have to offer. I'll try. That will be the best Christmas present I could give to you.

For your part, just keep being yourself. And please <u>be happy</u>. It is an act of the will you know; all else will take care of itself.

Lovingly,
Jim

Jim McCormick

CHRISTMAS 1985

We lack love's tolerance of faults

Dear Marilyn,

>It's Christmas Eve and here I sit,
>About to write a poem
>Reflecting on my life and love.
>Will it be a tome?

>This started many years ago
>When we were newly wed,
>An outgrowth of a need to say
>Just what was in my head.

>You liked my thoughts much better said
>On paper than with tongue,
>For love is easier to express
>In words that can be sung.

>And so a custom came to pass
>In which on Christmas Eve
>I tell you what I think of you
>And what I most believe.

>In years when harmony prevails
>And we have been a team
>My Christmas poem does write itself
>With ease so it would seem.

Story of a Marriage

In other years the strains of life
Play havoc with our love,
Dethrone the muse of former years
And still the turtle dove.
I have been known to write these words
As late as March or May,
When finally the ice went out
On heart as well as Bay.

So what of 1985?
The year we traveled west
Exploring in our vintage van
The mountains and the rest.

A year of tension with a son,
Of worry and of grief.
A year when joy and peaceful times
Were far too few and brief.

A year when news from Washington
Brought unexpected gloom
And anxious months awaiting a
Synthetic end to doom.

These things have put a strain upon
Two people merged as one.
And frequently we must have asked
"What happened to the fun?"

Jim McCormick

And tho our love survives these times
Because we choose to love,
We lack love's tolerance of faults,
A virtue from above.

I can't change you; you can't change me
But I will love you still
Because there's so much good in you.
Because I said "I will."

On Christmas Eve I wrote this poem
But couldn't finish it.
"Love and Duty," "Grin and Bear"
Just aren't by lovers writ.

And yet there are indeed those times
When spouses just can't swoon.
And Christmas 1985~~~~
No time, no loon, no moon.

I decided that I'd wait
Until the cloud would dissipate,
Revealing once again anew
What made me want to take a mate.

The cloud has lifted Valentine.
And once again I feel
The glow I felt when first we met,
The warmth of love that's real.

Story of a Marriage

I've missed you while you've been away
No one can take your place.
I love your look, your sound, your thoughts.
There's something about your face.

A belated Merry Christmas, 1985, Marilyn
Love, Jim

Jim McCormick

CHRISTMAS 1986

Things that made our lives full this year

Dear Marilyn,

Hiya Honey, Wifey, Mar, Sweetheart,

Okay I'll take your advice—I'm not going to talk about Dan. Not even about old Danny (our little dream boy of earlier days). I'm not going to remind you of anything which caused you pain in 1986. But I am going to use this Christmas letter to remind you of things that made our lives full and interesting and beautiful this year.

Life is never an unbroken song between turtle doves. Certainly ours isn't. But I am still glad I am sharing my life with you, after almost 19 years. It's been challenging and I've had to grow in unexpected and unwanted ways. You are a great lady, a woman of special depth and sensitivity. You have taught me a lot about life. You are, if anything, too perceptive. You are also a very loyal friend, especially to me. I get mad at you but I do love you and wouldn't want to be with anyone else.

I wish you were happier, for your sake. But that is something for you to work out. In the meantime I will strive to do what I can to make our path smoother.

Our big, long planned Florida excursion in April had some memorable surprises, didn't it? Like Fort Myers Beach. It was the second trip of the trilogy I laid out a few years ago—The West, The South, The East! Trips like that, accompanied by Danny, Ginny & David, will be treasured memories when we are old. Remember the three days at Disney World? What a concentration of sights and sounds in one place. Talking back and forth with Dick and Jeanette Dell'Acqua and their girls on the CB radio sure added to the enjoyment of the long drive. Remember "Red Dog" and "Godfather" and "Sara Belle" and "Tilly" and "The Judge" and the rest of our handles?

Hopefully we will have another and even greater family experience next summer when we take the kids and the old Dodge van on the last big trip, to New York, Washington and places East. You know I put a lot of my hopes and expectations into grand travel experiences like that, but I have to admit that our life is mainly composed of everyday activities in Traverse City, like turning off the alarm clock every morning at 7 AM, rousing the kids out of bed, making the first coffee, getting us all off to school and our jobs, getting everyone to their after school activities and sports, etc. Then there are our jobs, teaching and judging. Mine is very fulfilling and contributes wonderfully to my personal satisfaction in life. How about yours? I guess that is a psychological difference between most men and women. Your jobs don't mean so much to your level of contentedness.

I love you dearly honey, and just wish you greater serenity in your life, peace of mind and heart next year. You know our future is in God's hands. Let's concentrate on trusting our Great friend. Personally, I still think you are beautiful to behold. That's what got my attention almost 20 years ago in the church basement.

That and your wonderful enthusiasm.

Love,
Jim

Jim McCormick

CHRISTMAS 1987

A loving, committed marriage

Dear Marilyn,
Another year has gone by. What has changed other than our getting another year older? Are we better people for having spent another year living and trying to love, relating to people and trying to cope with the vicissitudes of life in the American world of stress, anxiety, constant change, opportunity, open-endedness, uncertainty, instability, self-centeredness, superficial concern for the under-privileged?

I don't know if you can measure progress in your own effort to become a better, more Christian human being? Maybe a year is too short a time. I personally don't feel any closer to God this year than last. And yet I think our introduction to a Bible study has put me in touch with His thinking, His way a bit more than before. The Little Rock scripture study has opened a better line of communication between us and the holy one. And that is a product of 1987. May it continue to bear fruit.

Our stressful relations with 17 year old Dan have dominated this otherwise peaceful year. Let us pray that, with God's help, Dan will find his way to maturity and peace of mind this next year, as he and we prepare for his entry into adulthood.

Because your distress over Dan's attitude and rebelliousness has so often spilled over into our marital relationship, I have overlooked the positive side of our family life. Looking beyond our temporary parent-teenager conflict, I can see we still have a loving, committed marriage, that we are a team in our approach to the world, that I admire and respect and enjoy and love you very much. You, for your part, are a tower of strength in your steadfast loyalty to me and to your family and friends. Your humanities work in the C.M.U. master's degree program has been an enriching experience in your life. So all will be well and we will have better times ahead. Go to bed content in the knowledge that your Jim loves you very much.

Jim

CHRISTMAS 1988

The big blessing of the year

Dear Marilyn,

This is going to be a short Christmas letter because I put it off until today (Christmas Eve) and I am writing at Mom & Dad's apartment. Mom doesn't give anyone much peace and quiet for thinking and writing.

Her senility and Dad's frailty are a major concern of ours this year. They seem fated to stay together in this apartment until one of them has to go to a hospital for something serious. I just hope it doesn't end in some kind of very painful experience for one of them. I want you to know how much I appreciate your kindness and encouragement to them these last few years. I hope I am as good to your folks when time catches up to them.

It's been an interesting year for us. Lots of worry, followed by lots of growth, ending on a positive note. We won't forget the emptiness of Dan's graduation. Little did we realize just how much in trouble he was. But the culmination of his alcohol and drug abuse was the Munson treatment program, which has been the big blessing of the year for us all. Whatever Dan may do, we will all be much better able to deal with it in the future. We all have the tools for successful living and are using them, or trying to. No more fear!

As I observe my Dad's dedicated care for my Mom I am impressed with the power of a commitment for life. We have the same commitment. We may argue and get irritated, but we are a pair for life. That is a very comforting thought.

There isn't anything we haven't talked about over these past 20 years. I trust you completely. I am comfortable with you and wouldn't want to be with anyone else. In the 20 years we have been married I have never fantasized being married to anyone else. I am proud of you and proud to be your husband. And I love you. Looking forward to another year.

Love

Jim

Jim McCormick

CHRISTMAS 1989

A comfortable life, thanks to you

Dear Marilyn,
Writing cards tonight. Typical weekday evening. David doing homework after calling to show concern to Erin Schmuckal who he clumsily tripped today. Ginny coming in late, from Xmas party at the Omelette Shop. Dan's not home from Loyola University until Friday. You recuperating on the couch in the sitting room from a long day at St. Francis High. Me—putzing around after reading every last page of the Record Eagle, including obituaries. A comfortable life. Thanks to you and your carefully laid plans.

I love you,
Jim

CHRISTMAS 1990

Our growing commitment to each other

Dear Marilyn,
Another Christmas. This one in Detroit. Danny in Europe. Ginny home from State. David just being David. Middle age upon us. You have been feeling it this year. I fight it and act like it isn't here yet. But the changes all around us say time is marching on. There are great grandchildren around. Not ours! But the very idea is startling. Two of our three are off to college. Our routine will change. So far these changes have been easy and pleasant. Yet we see the slow decline of our parents and aunts and uncles. It prepares us for a consciousness of mortality ... and immortality. I become more conscious of the tenacity of our relationship, our long-enduring marriage, our growing commitment to marriage as an institution which is so crucial to our civilization, and our growing commitment to each other. I become much more grateful to you for saying yes 23 years ago, for casting your lot with me, for taking a chance on me. I thank you for your gritty friendship, for your strength of character, for your bringing out the best in me.
   I love you much,
   Jim

Jim McCormick

THANK YOU MARILYN FOR BEING CHRIST TO ME

Christ, the integrating principle
In a life of change invincible.
Tho middle age spins right and left
With Jesus no danger of hope bereft.

My hope is in God, the big picture.
Mid turmoil, the one sure fixture.
But you, Marilyn, bring down to Earth
His promise of love and rebirth.

With kids off to State and to Rome,
And parents to the old folks home;
Lives of promise and lives slowing down,
You are my constant, my ground.

I thank you, Marilyn, for saying "yes,"
For 23 years of love, no less.
I'm honored and humbled by your steadfast love,
My sign of the eternal love Jesus spoke of.

CHRISTMAS 1991

*An inordinate craving for tranquility
in my family*

Dear Marilyn, my wife of nearly 24 years,
Tonight, as I write this, you are not feeling very upbeat. In fact, you are downright depressed. My inclination is to try to sell you on the many reasons to feel optimistic about life. But from experience I know that wouldn't work. I have an inordinate craving for peace and tranquility in my family.

Why am I starting my annual Christmas letter to you on this disturbing note? I guess it is because, in all honesty, it is much on my mind. When I imagine this temperamental imbalance between us may last "'til death do us part," I am discouraged. At such times I am tempted to withdraw into myself and deal with you on a friendly but superficial level, protecting my own vulnerable ego.

I don't believe you empathize with my reaction because you never acknowledge it. How could you? My sensitivity to your agitation seems exaggerated and inappropriate to you.

To me it seems that you need outside help with your underlying chronic anger, while you probably think I need help with my inordinate need for peace and quiet.

What a dilemma! You are unhappy with me and with the kids and with your own family and with yourself often. I can either engage your anger, which I do, with negative results or I can detach from the fray, which I am tempted to but don't want to do. Detachment seems cowardly and ultimately would lead to emotional separation. I would rather that we become soulmates again, as we once were.

I love you very much and always will. I long for the closeness we had during most of our nearly 24 years of this marriage. Maybe nothing will change until you are a few years older and no longer dealing with the kids as subordinates. I can wait it out but it would sure be nice to find a way to be happy consistently now. Not that we don't have days, or weeks of harmony now. We do. But these are now the exception. At such times you come alive and are a different person. You don't constantly find fault with everything David (or Ginny or Danny when they are home) do or fail to do. It's wonderful. During these times you get angry once in a while, not all the time.

If we love each other, and I know we do, we should do something to try to resolve our problems. Maybe the best investment we could make would be meeting several times with a marriage counselor. We need someone with concrete suggestions. Maybe the Marriage Encounter weekend will get us started, but I think we need counseling too. Somebody to test our different versions of reality and show us our blind spots.

Let's not let our love suffer from the strain which is on it. Why waste time, hoping the situation will correct itself. Let's tackle this obstacle to our marital bliss more aggressively. You can count on me to tough it out, and I know I can trust you to do the same, but maybe with an outsider's insights and expertise we can resolve this and be happier now.

We are nearing that magic 25th anniversary. Let's set a goal of being soulmates again before that day arrives. You are by far the main person in my life and I want to do what it takes to be happier together. I feel that if you become a happier person your anger will subside and I automatically will be happier, as I am codependent on your moods.

I recognized your inner beauty as soon as we met, and I have never had a second thought about that. I was also attracted to your physical beauty, of course, but I saw your intelligence, your leadership, your loyalty to your friends, your intuition, your depth. You haven't lost your face, and you have only grown in all these other ways.

We have many years to travel together. Let's not settle for less intimacy and compatibility than is possible for us. This letter may not compete with Browning and Rosetti, but it comes from my heart as we approach the end of the year 1991.

Love, kisses and a Merry Christmas at the Torina party.
Jim

Jim McCormick

CHRISTMAS 1992

A feeling you were the woman I was looking for

Dear Marilyn,

For a change I am not writing your Christmas letter in the attic bedroom at Grand Marais on Christmas Eve, desperately working against the clock as your dad calls me to the late night celebration. I am actually sitting in the sitting room at home in the big, comfortable chair, with my feet up. I just figured out how to get the CD player to work for the first time. A Christmas album is playing "We Three Kings." Sounds like an omen calling us to the Star in Bethlehem. Maybe we should follow that star (with a side trip to Egypt or Constantinople, of course).

My apologies for the unimaginative stationery this year. We didn't bring any back from the Black Hills in June, so I have nothing more exotic to use.

Well, back to today! It's a beautiful, cold early winter morning. Something got settled at the last minute so I don't start court at 8:30 today. I have an hour to donate to saying something I might not otherwise say to you. Of course, with our new attention to dialoging on our love letters, we have communicated more deeply than in the past. Our October Marriage Encounter may turn out to be the most valuable thing we did in 1992. I hope so.

Now the disc is playing "Oh Holy Night," which brings me to the subject of this letter. While driving home last night my mind wandered to the night we met, almost 26 years ago. It was a momentous night, a holy night. I had a feeling right away that something special was happening, that you were the woman I was looking for. (And you were.)

What was it that so attracted me to you? It was a lot of things in one person. First the externals. The way you carried yourself. Like some well-bred princess from Africa. Tall, slim, angular, attractively clothed, your hair just right, just enough makeup. Then it was your features. High cheekbones, chiseled jaw, aquiline nose, noble brow, fine, perfectly shaped mouth, big almond shaped eyes. You were just friendly enough towards a strange man to whom you were being introduced by a mutual friend. No fuss, no gush, just a friendly interest. You immediately engaged me in conversation which had some meaning. It was during a break in a program about race relations, and racial justice in Detroit. We were in the basement of St. Clare Church. There was a large crowd. You were sitting across the hall with Jean. I was with Jerry. We all got together over coffee during the intermission. Within that ten minute period I knew I wanted to pursue my interest in making you my wife!

I couldn't wait for the rest of the program to end so we could pick up where we left off.

And we did, over at my house. As we all discussed racial justice for another couple hours I became convinced that my interest in you surpassed just wanting to date you. I felt I had met a kindred spirit. Someone with whom my ideals and goals in life had a real chance of being realized. I also was coming to appreciate your quick mind, your ability to think ahead, your split second analysis of a situation, almost always right on point. Your giftedness!

Temperamentally and in terms of the way we think or approach things we are like Arabs and Jews, as opposite as conceivable. Yet we share a universe of common ideas, values, goals. We proceed so differently towards the same destinations. We are both complementary and contrary in the way we approach life psychologically. I think we help each other more than we know. It is easy to see how our styles of thinking lead to conflict. It is not so readily obvious that our divergence in strengths and weaknesses serves to protect us both from extremes.

Well, the Christmas CD just ended and my letter is coming to a finish, too. After 25 years we are still working out our complex relationship of psychological opposites with identical values, goals and interests, both strong-willed.

You are still that young African princess with the noble carriage and face to match. (I say African because I picture a serene, proud girl from a tribal kingdom, with natural, inherited grace and poise.) I know I got a winner, a princess, a proud beauty, a serious woman who is determined to import knowledge and wisdom to her students! A scrupulously honest participant in St. Francis High School's efforts to make a difference in young lives. A fierce mother who looks out for her three children all the time. A super-<u>loyal</u> wife who never criticizes her husband's work although you must sometimes disagree with what I do.

For all these reasons I truly love you, Marilyn, and look forward to the next 25 years with you.

Love and Merry Christmas,

Jim

CHRISTMAS 1993

How different your psyche is from mine

Dear Marilyn,

In December of 1968 I wrote a Christmas letter to you. You liked the idea and declared it a "tradition," and this it has become. Sometimes late and occasionally strained, but always delivered. These letters probably say more about me than they do about you, as they reflect the year as I have experienced it. Sometimes struggling to find something to say about a hard year for our little ship.

Looking at the "State of the Union," 1993, I realize that my assessment depends upon perspective. It has been a struggle for you because of the tenaciousness of your depression this year. In other ways it has been a wonderful year. Dan, Ginny and David are maturing as young adults we can be very proud of. Our professional lives have been fulfilling. Our saga in the Holy Land and Constantinople-Istanbul this summer was an experience of a lifetime. We are surrounded by old friends. Our families are close, as always.

Then there is us—you and me. I feel closer to you than ever before. I am becoming more understanding of you and therefore more empathetic. I have come to appreciate just how radically different your psyche is from mine. How you suffer through things which come so easily to me.

Whatever the cause, I feel closer to you, wishing to shelter you from harm but not knowing how. I want to cuddle you and make you feel safe and good about yourself and the world. It's so sad that you lack an appreciation of what a fine person you are. I look forward to the day when you can finally come to terms with yourself and relax and be happy.

This year you have added your Masters Degree in Humanities to your years of being an acknowledged master teacher. I am proud of you. You should be proud of you. Thanks for being a great life partner.

Love & Merry Christmas,

Jim

CHRISTMAS 1994

Wanting to be your most intimate friend

Dear Darling Marilyn,
Eureka! I have found help in avoiding conflicts with sweet, loving damsels in distress (meaning you). Of course I am speaking of the BOOK: *Men are from Mars, Women are from Venus*. Reading this book on our camping trips, reading aloud to you from it, discussing it with you and our dinner group all have given me a great infusion of hope that we can be a <u>really</u> happy couple. I've always regretted that our strong personalities seemed to clash too often, leaving both of us angry & resentful and frustrated. Small differences would escalate into arguments.

With effort, goodwill and mutual love, all of which we have, we can aspire to the experience of real harmony, which has often eluded us. I am very excited about this because I want our relationship to be the most treasured part of our lives, a wellspring of love we can share with others, starting with our children, family and friends, not to mention the whole human race.

I love you very much, Marilyn, and really want to be your most intimate friend until death do us part. After all, you are beautiful, smart, kind and mine.

Love and Merry Christmas,
Jim

P.S. Congratulations on the Masters Degree in Humanities, CMU, '94

Photo Addendum

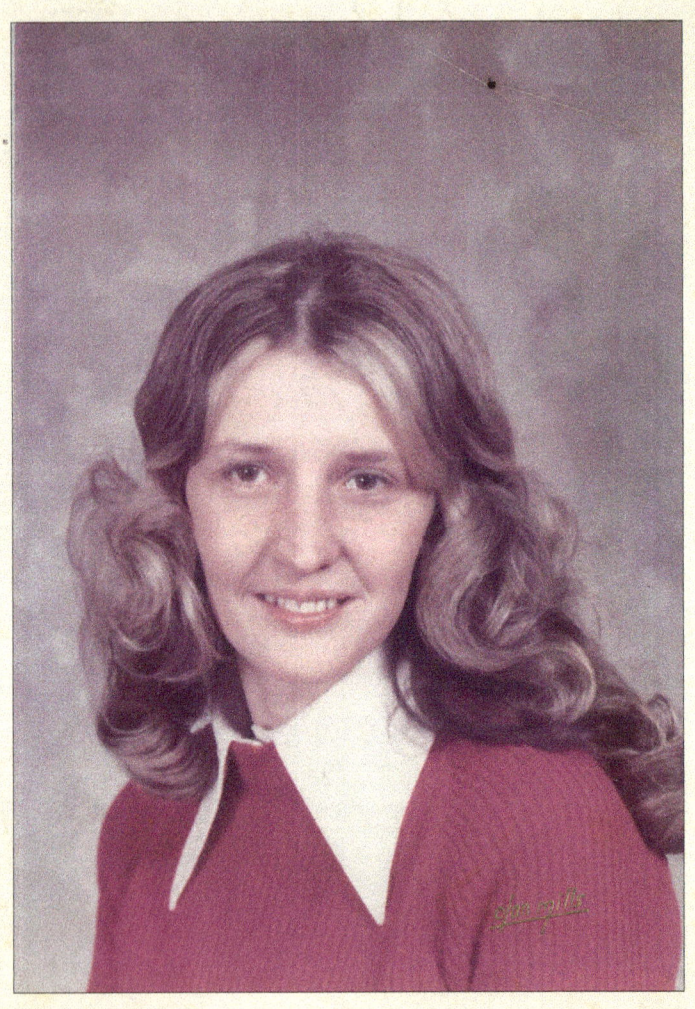

Marilyn, about 28, taken by a photographer friend.

Judicial election campaign picture, 1976.

Me "babysitting" Dan, David, and Ginny. Christmas, 1976.

Portrait of Marilyn as a young wife and mother. Painted by a friend of ours. My Christmas present to Marilyn, about 1978.

With our three kids. From left: David, Ginny, Dan.
Watercolor. My 1981 Christmas present to Marilyn.
Done by a local painter.

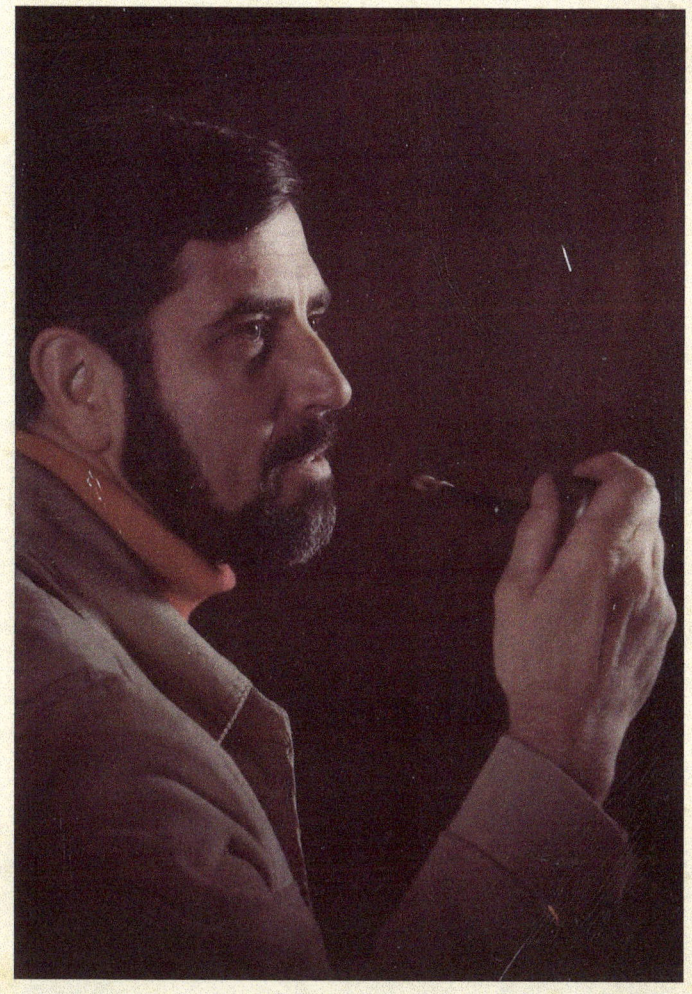

Judicial election campaign photo, 1982. Trying to look "wise," I guess.

The five of us at the Japanese Tea Garden in San Francisco. During our great family road trip Out West, summer of 1985.

Photo of Marilyn, taken at our 25th anniversary party, 1993. I kiss a framed enlargement of it in my front hallway as I come and go.

Proud parents in California for David's graduation from Middlebury Institute of International Studies at Monterey, 2004.

Us on the rocky shore of Lake Superior, our favorite retreat after the kids were on their own.

Us, in a reflective moment, two weeks before she died.

Marilyn's tombstone. Tells it all.

Middle Age Marriage 1995–2000

~~~~~~

CHRISTMAS 1995

Your zest for life and passion for truth

Dear Marilyn, My love:
It's Christmas Eve 1995, time for me to review the year's events and offer a few suggestions for <u>your</u> self-improvement! Constructive suggestions of course, and presented as subtly as possible.

No, I'm not going to go that route this year. Instead, this letter will be an unadulterated tribute, an homage, to your virtue and your beauty. I have learned my lesson! (Just kidding.)

Readers of this genre (a la Robert Browning to Elizabeth Barrett, Dante Gabriel Rossetti to Christina Rosetti) fifty years from now, take note that this was the year of the angel. See angelic scene on the front of the card.

You Marilyn, are that angel in the flesh. A creature filled with the sparks of divinity, living on an elevated plane, feet on earth but head in the heavens! I thank your ancestors for giving you the facial beauty which first captured my attention. You have retained it all these years. I thank you for your zest for life and your passion for truth and friendship. You are very lovable.

You are cordially invited to be my guest from Friday evening, January 26 until Sunday afternoon, January 28, 1996, as a guest of Herman's Cafe and European Hotel, Cadillac, Michigan. Our usual room awaits our arrival.

Merry Christmas,

Jim

Jim McCormick

CHRISTMAS 1996

Your beautiful smile on your flawless face

Dear Marilyn,
Just to keep you off guard; this is not going to be a rehash of the year, but a more feeling-touchy kind of Christmas letter. Perhaps even impressionistic!

I am downright proud to be penning these lines on Wednesday, December 18th in the courthouse rather than the usual last ditch effort performed up in the attic bedroom at Grand Marais on December 24 at 10:00 PM.

Well here goes.

Let me take this occasion to tell you in writing, which can be reread all year, that I still feel the way about you that I felt when we were first married. Only now I know better why. I love your zest for life and your warmth with people, and I love you for those qualities. I love your beautiful smile on your flawless face. I love your sincerity and your dedication to what you believe, and I love you for those qualities. I love your sense of humor, which expands with the years. I love the way you love me, which is so generous and unjustified. I love you for sharing uniquely with me our steadfast and passionate love for our children and our all-absorbing interest in their welfare and future.

I love you also in ways only explained by the term "chemistry." You are right for me, and I think and hope I am right for you. I thank God our loving Parent for bringing us together in the basement of St. Clare Church in 1967, almost 30 years ago. We should celebrate that anniversary this March 14.

I love to cuddle up to you all night while you watch t.v. and I vacillate between listening and trying to go to sleep. I love the way you care about your students and the way you know how to help them and to say the right thing to them when they need guidance. I like being allied to your efforts, which are building the Kingdom of God every day.

I thoroughly enjoy our repartee on a multitude of topics, especially since you seem to be finally coming to appreciate my Irish wit rather than taking it as sarcasm.

Let us pray that the Good Lord will give us many more good years together.

Merry Christmas,

Jim

Jim McCormick

CHRISTMAS 1997

Time to enjoy the golden years with you

Dear Marilyn—Honey—Sweetheart,
I have kept this stationery since 1993 for just such an occasion as this—my annual Christmas love letter. I am sure you recall Hotel Stella at Kusadasi, Turkey with good memories. That was the most enjoyable place for you on that trip. The weather was mild, the scenery romantic, and you became instant friends with an American tourist lady from Texas—a soulmate. I was just happy that you were happy after many days of heat prostration.

Lots of water has gone over our dam since that trip to the Middle East. I have found a major new interest—the Holy Land, and you have put an end to many years of full-time teaching. I hope and pray your decision leads you to other fulfilling roles. I am sure it will. Sometimes I worry about what you will do to satisfy your need to contribute your talent to people.

I am proud of your accomplishments as a teacher. The protracted testimonial to your contributions to St. Francis High School at this Fall's Academic Banquet made my heart swell with pride and also with gratitude that you were getting the recognition you deserve.

As we move closer, day by day, to the time when neither of us will be going off to a job every morning, I have some trepidation but mainly I look forward to having time to enjoy the golden years with you. It will take a bit of compromising but I expect we will have a very full life for years and years to come. Our three dear children and their future families will play a big part in our plans. But at the heart of it will be our love and commitment to each other, just as it was in 1968. Looking forward to the big 30th anniversary.

Much love and kisses,

Jim

CHRISTMAS 1998

As our children inch closer to their future

Dear Marilyn,
Merry Christmas and a wonderful second last year of the second millennium of the Church of Jesus Christ.

I am excited about our forthcoming trip to England. As the poet Browning said, "Oh to be in England now that April's here." Also our weekend at Staffords Inn at Bay View for Valentine's Day. That's one of your Christmas gifts. And I hope you like the amber pendant and chain. It's from the Baltic.

As our three beloved children inch closer to their future lives and we have less responsibility for their welfare, I see us moving into a time of freedom to do what we please, and I know we will please to do many fulfilling things together. I am glad you are my partner in life.

Love,
Jim

JANUARY 1999

Note to me while in the Holy Land

My dearest Jim,
I know you are having a wonderful time because you are a person whose capacity for wonder hasn't diminished with age. I guess our wholeness comes from merging our lives.

"Love is the passionate and abiding desire on the part of two people to produce <u>together</u> conditions under which each can be, and spontaneously express, his/her <u>real</u> <u>self</u>. To produce together an intellectual soil and an emotional climate in which each can flourish, far superior to what either could achieve alone."

We must be in love! Hurry home!
All my love,
Marilyn

Jim McCormick

CHRISTMAS in GEORGIA, 2000
(excerpts from a journal written to Marilyn from Georgia)

I concentrate on your face as I write here in Georgia

Dear Marilyn,
This journal is in place of my usual Christmas letter. So visualize that I am thinking of <u>you</u> and speaking to <u>you</u>. I can't believe I am experiencing serenity about this mission to the Republic of Georgia, where Christmas is in mid January. Last week I was very anxious about living with a Georgian family in Tbilisi, thinking they would speak little English. What was I going to have to contribute to the presentations to Georgian audiences about the worldwide tragedy of domestic violence, and our ideas for reducing it.

Before I close my eyes to take a nap on this Lufthansa flight from Boston to Frankfurt I want to tell you I am thinking of you, feeling love for you, and very much wishing you were here to share whatever is on the horizon.

Now here I am on an Airzena Georgia flight to the Georgian capital, Tbilisi! This is the real thing! Most of the people aboard are obviously Georgian. Black hair, dark eyes, big eyes, prominent noses. Very robust-looking people. Reminds me of Romanians (other side of the Black Sea). Goodnight honey.

Story of a Marriage

It's Sunday morning in Tbilisi, 10:45 AM here, 1:45 AM there. You are sleeping. I hope you are comfortable. No leg cramps or heebegeebees. David being home from Brazil must still be a lift for you and a comfort too.

We just had breakfast downstairs in this little guest house. The six of us were the only people present. We occupy all six rooms.

Tomorrow we meet our host families. Today we ate two splendid tables of Eastern dishes you would go crazy over.

As I doze off I will be visualizing you, Marilyn. It is 1:00 PM in Traverse City. I hope your day is going well. Give my love to all, especially to yourself.

It's 10:00 PM and I am again getting ready to go to bed, this time in the <u>only</u> bedroom in the apt of Nika, Maka, and toddler Lika, my hosts for the next two weeks.

One day at a time! Thinking fond thoughts of you and wishing you were here to carry the conversation. I promise I will never again growl about you talking too much. Your effervescent style is sorely missed here. Love and kisses. It's Monday night.

Jim McCormick

~~~~~

Just as I was becoming comfortable I started to feel nauseated yesterday. I shouldn't have eaten supper here at all. I went to sleep at 10:00 PM and awakened at 2:00 AM with diarrhea. Even got quite a bit on my pajamas, which I washed out in the unlit bathroom. Up again at 6:30 AM this time much worse, followed by prolonged vomiting. Nika and Maka can't imagine why, as they cook everything fresh.

Our presentations to social agencies in the morning and Police Academy instructors in the afternoon went well.

Maka Makchaneli came over to meet me last night. She was part of the 1989–1991 city exchanges between Mahketa, Georgia and Traverse City. I also feel your vibes, honey, and they give me strength and confidence that I will get through this thrilling experience.

What are you doing? What is Dave up to? Are his plans shaping up? Are you giving him space? Is Dan calling regularly? I'll be bringing wine for Gin and Darric and probably costume jewelry for you and something like Georgian hats for Dan and David. Not too exciting, except for the wine.

I wish you were here to do the shopping. I promise I would accept your judgment! Good night, sweet lady.

It's cold in this apt. I have two shirts on and am under two blankets (one a thick tick). The bedding is quite comfortable; it's just that there is very little heat in the building. Tonight the water is too cold to even think about a shower. Nika and Maka do everything possible to accommodate my queasy stomach, but are chafing at the bit to show me a real big meal.

Marilyn, I concentrate on your face as I sit here under the covers. Georgian women can be plain or very pretty, but none so far are as beautiful as you. Of course few women have your classic good looks combined with that look of intelligence and savoir faire. You would truly enjoy the variety of dishes here. Nicely spiced. Lots of veggies, usually mashed with nuts on top. I wish I could adequately describe them. I spend so many hours every day in ice cold buildings, very barren and dank and drafty, listening to others of our team lecturing before it is finally my turn. I am always last, and often rushed. The same talks get boring and contribute to my sleeplessness. I hope my email has reached you by now. It was short and to the point.

This AM we spoke to psychiatrists and psychologists who work with people traumatized by war, terror, refugee status, etc. There are 350,000 internal refugees in Georgia, kicked out of the province of Abkhazia on the Black Sea by the Muslim minority acting with Russian help. The audience was almost all women. Supposedly very Freudian in their old soviet training. All in all, some unique experiences. Love and kisses. I love you. Until tomorrow, sweetheart.

Marilyn, I long to see you and rest in your arms and talk all about the borders of Central Asia in the wintertime. Thank God we were not born in this very hard world where life is such a struggle for these good people. May the Lord bring them prosperity.

I realize this hasn't seemed very personal but I am thinking of you as I write and feel like I am talking to you. I hope you aren't too bored by these details. This is an intense few weeks and it's important to me that you get the full flavor of what I am experiencing (going through). There are still another five days of teaching (or speaking to groups) so I am a long way from completing my responsibilities. I can see the light at the end of the tunnel, though, and just can't wait to fall asleep in our bed. For now, I love you and hope and pray all is going well with you, Ginny and Darric, David and Dan and all our many friends, and I pray your colonoscopy, etc. is easy and results are the picture of health.

We spent part of today eating, eating, drinking, drinking, talking back and forth in Georgian and some translating for me and of my words to them. Many toasts. They love to eat and drink and make wonderful toasts to everybody and everything. I have to work at this, but the results are okay. They like me and give off very good vibes. Marilyn, you would hate the cold rooms and infrequent electricity and little balky cars and gray apartment blocks and potholes, but you would do so much better at the human side of this than I can ever do.

The women of your age group I've met are invariably charming, gracious, natural, well-groomed, a little plump and love to serve their specialties. You would love the multiple dishes on every table, all beautifully displayed and interesting. Half the time I don't know what I'm eating, not a situation I relish. You would ask questions, get some recipes, etc. Some dishes seem to have a Persian origin, some Turkish, some Russian or Armenian, and the majority true Georgian.

I love you and think of you all the time and wonder how you are doing at night and your health and energy. I just discovered that I forgot all about David's birthday (yesterday). I bought you a Russian cameo/gold ring today. It looks like you. I hope you like it. Lots of gold, supposedly 9 grams. I think it was quite a bargain, considering the value of gold. It would be hard to return it. So goodnight, sweet love. Sweet dreams.

Had a pretty good day today. Our presentation to a human rights organization this AM and to army officers this afternoon went well. Love, love, love to all but particularly to the love of my life. Only fools and Project Harmony would pick January to spend in Georgia, but we have survived!! Praise the Lord. Goodnight, Love.

At long last we are ready to return home. Two months since Project Harmony called and asked me to work on this mission in Georgia! It has been on my mind a lot, especially since my retirement became official a month ago. I have often felt a little like Marco Polo when he passed along this Silk Road on his way to China. He must have been quite a man.

I miss you as always and can't wait to drive you crazy with monologues about my experiences. You can't stand still long for those mandatory purgatives.

I have said my goodbyes to a lot of people tonight at the big farewell banquet. Many wine toasts. I led my share. I am tired and need to go to sleep, so I will end this journal by telling you again that I have missed you but have felt your presence every day. Everything I have seen and done would have been better if shared with you. I love you and can't wait to see you at the T.C. airport tomorrow afternoon. I will also look forward to seeing Ginny, Darric, Dave, Dan and anyone else who I have missed.

It's now Christmas in Georgia's next door neighbor, Armenia. So I can still wish you a belated Merry Christmas.

Love, Jim

Early Retirement
2001–2010

CHRISTMAS 2001

I will support your dream

Dear beloved Marilyn, love of my life, partner of my days, mistress of my house, mother of my children, backer of my dreams and inspiration of all my plans:

It is almost midnight, Christmas Eve, as I write these words, so I will spare you my take on all the year's events, even though I know how you loved those rambling Christmas letters of past years in which I gave a run-down of every up and down of our lives. (Not so?)

This has been one of those turning point years as we have adjusted our schedules and our habits to accommodate my retirement.

I think we have done that exceedingly well. You have had the knack of rearranging the house itself so I feel comfortable being around more of the time. I thank you for that. My "office" has been a big success. I love working down here.

We have also had a great deal of fun traveling this year, taking full advantage of our new leisure time. The camping trip to the South was hard for you, as you weren't feeling very well, but you bravely went ahead for my sake. The camping trip to Canada was an unmixed blessing, as everything came together. I got an idea as to how much enjoyment we can have traveling over the years to come. You were a great sport. Onward to Alaska?

Then there was our shared experience in Italy, particularly the nine days in Sicily. It was a pleasure for me to watch you bloom on the island of your ancestors. Your excitement was wonderful to behold. Your passion to return there for a longer stay will give you another raison d'etre. I will support your dream.

I continue to love you very much and wish you a great Christmas and New Year.

Love,

Jim

CHRISTMAS 2002

Our meeting has elevated my life

Dear Marilyn,

I just had a thought which I want to pass along to you at Christmas. How and why I happened to have this thought, I am not sure. It just came to me, out of the blue, as my mind was wandering during a trial.

The thought is this: Whatever I am at this time in my life I owe to you. The direction in which my life has gone is in great part attributable to your influence, your personality, your values, your lifestyle. Without you, my life would have gone in some unknown direction. I feel sure our meeting has elevated my life to a high dimension. Thanks sweetheart.

Love and a Merry Christmas,
Jim

CHRISTMAS 2003

You need a life saver, and I throw you a line of advice

Dear Marilyn,

I could start off my Christmas letter with some family bragging about the delivery of our first grandchild, Cameron Andrew Newman to Ginny and Darric. Then David's graduation from Monterey Institute with his Masters in Linguistics. But you don't want a recitation of the news of the year, so I'll get personal.

First of all, I want you to know how much I love you, my special lifetime partner. You have always been my biggest booster and most loyal friend. Even when you are mad at me there is no doubt in my mind that you are emotionally committed. I am always secure about your friendship and loyalty and commitment.

Today at Karen and J's Christmas Eve party, you were at your vivacious best, entertaining everyone in the room with your laugh, your joie de vivre, and your well-told stories. You were so much pure fun.

Even in your down moods you keep playing along like a trooper, never quitting. I know you endure a lot of pain at those times. You need a life saver, and I often throw you a line of advice instead. For that I am very sorry. Maybe I will learn to give you the simple support of a sympathetic ear.

We are at a new stage of life, the early retirement years, ideally some of the best years of life, a time for greater freedom of action and fewer responsibilities. I look forward to 2004 and many more years of sharing my life with you. I just hope I can master the art of loving you more selflessly, because I know that opens up your great big heart.

Friday we go to Laguna Niguel with Dave to visit Dan. Another adventure. We just got off the phone with Gin. We are fortunate to have three wonderful children. And hasn't it been a pleasure living at Jerry's place? We are blessed. Praise the Lord Jesus on his birthday.

Much love,

Jim

CHRISTMAS 2004

We have metamorphosed into who we truly are

Dear Marilyn,

Our love is truly "lifelong." That we can say after nearly 40 years. Actually love was blossoming in the autumn of 1967. Remember when we traveled up here to Leelanau County to see the fall colors? How could we know we would live the rest of our lives here?

Thales, the first Greek philosophical thinker of note, would dispute that our love, or anything is "lifelong," since "panta rei" (everything continually is in a state of change). He would say you cannot put your foot in a river twice, because both you and the ever-flowing river will have changed, become something else.

Yes, it is true that neither you nor I are the <u>same</u> as when we began, but I would say we have kept our relationship growing as we and our personalities have grown, and metamorphosed into who we are today. I renew my commitment to the ever-changing and fascinating you.

Love,
Jim

CHRISTMAS 2005

The prospect of letting go of things of the world while holding hands

Merry Christmas Marilyn, my lifelong lover.
Today is Tuesday, December 13, 2005, with snow so deep, and I begin this year's installment of the Christmas expression of my love.

I am at one of my favorite new haunts, Another Cup of Joe, a strangely romantic and evocative, yet laid back little coffee house, where one feels liberated and free to express feelings. Once a hippy at heart, always, I guess.

I'm feeling particularly exhilarated today, like all is right with the world. For my prevailing state of bliss I have you, dad and his genes to thank. You, for supporting me in everything I have ever sought to do or be, for being my loyal believer and reality check, for being willing to go along with my dreams, ambitions and wander lust for these 38 years.

There are a million people, places and things I have come to know and love in this riotously fascinating world. Thank God, I have been given the gift of detachment, so I do not fear losing possession of them, being confident we will all be reunited in eternal life.

The prospect, at age 71, of letting go, ever so slowly, of the beautiful transient things of this world, while holding hands, figuratively and in the flesh, with you, dear, as your youthful type of beauty matures towards a more spiritual goodness, makes me want to leap forward with the anticipation of a child at dawn on Christmas Day. Anticipation of gifts we haven't even imagined, gifts of the heart, hidden lovingly under the Christmas tree of life.

Ad multos annos,

Jim

Jim McCormick

CHRISTMAS 2006

Oriental Wedding Song
(David and Ji-eun's wedding in Korea)

I.
Come Marilyn let's look at this year as we two
Have been blessed with abundant good health.
Two thousand and six was a year when we knew
An adventure worth more than great wealth.

REFRAIN:
Let us recall this year, when hope shall be tested
by fear.
(repeat)

II.
How off to the ends of the earth we did soar
With Jerry and Margy and Dan.
To a land we could only imagine, before
David's love for Lee Ji-eun began.

REFRAIN:
Let us recall this year, when hope shall be tested
by fear.
(repeat)

III.
How sweet was the love we beheld in our son
Toward the doll he has chosen for life.
A love that is Asian-Caucasian-Eurasian.
Confirmed by the glance of his wife.

~~~~~

REFRAIN:
Let us recall this year, when hope shall be tested
by fear.
(repeat)

IV.
Remember the crowds on the streets of Hong Kong,
The Han River in Seoul, and Kyong-ju?
We have shared, you and I, in adventure headlong,
Our bond strengthened by fun, and love too.

~~~~~

FINAL REFRAIN:
Let us recall this year, and drink some good cheer,
my dear.
(repeat)

Love and Happy Korean Christmas. Jim

CHRISTMAS 2007

My mood is muted by your seasonal melancholy

Dear Loving Wife Marilyn Frances,

My "Christmas letter" to you, a tradition going on forty years. I well remember that first Christmas after our 1968 wedding. For some reason I penned a love letter, telling you what our new life together meant to me. To my surprise, you fell in love with the idea of an annual Christmas letter, and prevailed upon me to make it a tradition.

Over the years the "letter" has waxed and waned. In some years a short, frank love letter. Sometimes a bit more creative. More often a laborious chronicle of the year's momentous events, along the lines of the Domesday Book of the early Middle Ages, as in the following episode:

> "In the year of our Lord 992 the fearsome, red-headed Norse barbarians invaded again our suffering shores. They came in great ships, the likes of which we had not seen before but had heard of in their songs. They were armed with swords and metal shields which no christian peasant can resist. They were clothed like bears, with long metal horns on their helmets. Our garrison was, of course, overwhelmed, and our strongest warriors disemboweled. Only a pitiful group of women and children survive.
>
> Christ Jesus, come quickly to rescue your people!"

Of course there have been a few inspired years, producing poems and even a song or two. Last year I out-did myself with that ode to our adventure trip to the exotic world of Korea for David's wedding to Lee Ji-eun, our beloved new daughter-in-law.

This Christmas my mood is slightly muted by your seasonal melancholy, which seems stronger than in past years. I certainly cannot talk you out of it. The best I can do is support you emotionally and remind myself why I look forward to the Christmas season every year.

You are entertaining Father Andy, Jack, Jan and Tak Ready tomorrow. You have been planning the menu for days, if not weeks now, and with loving care. Is this not the Christmas Spirit? You will put your all into creating a festive Christmas Dinner for people we love, and who might not be able to enjoy such a warm, good time without you devoting yourself to their enjoyment. You have also put a lot of loving thought into Christmas gift shopping for all the family, inspired by the story of the Three Kings. You should realize that you are piercing the gloom and, in your own way, helping the Good news of Christ's coming to alter the immortal destiny of the human race. Because of Him our destiny is unending fulfillment, happiness, joy, loving kindness in the company of love Him-Her-Self and a perfected creation. No suffering, no death, no pain, no sorrow; only selfless love towards God and others. Our heart's desire.

I love you Marilyn Torina, and want you to experience my joy and enthusiasm about the great future that lies ahead. I struggle to remember that only empathy positively affects you. I will try to be more supportive when you are down. That would be my best Christmas gift to you.

Love, Jim

~~~~~~~~~~~~~~~

And Merry Christmas

P.S. I hope you like the new setting for your engagement ring. And be sure to keep open the evening of Friday, January 11 and the next morning.

CHRISTMAS 2008

*Happy with you I am, and you are
most responsible*

Dear Marilyn,

It's Saturday night, the 20th of December in the year 2008, and the clock just (proverbially) struck nine. You have retired quite early, unusual for the night owl you are. You are no doubt enjoying one of your favorite TV programs or a movie, or the latest coverage of the activities of President-Elect Barack Obama.

For my part I am relaxing in the quiet of the kitchen. I have completed and checked off my mental list of pre-Christmas musts: writing notes on forty cards, stringing outdoor lights, a modicum of shopping, washing your soot-covered car, participating in a frenzy of emails between Toronto, Sao Paulo, Charlevoix and Traverse City, prompted by the passport/visa crisis of our dear Biel's son Mauricio, who is due to arrive tomorrow for a weeklong visit with us. Finally, I have been on the internet for hours, checking out hotels and B&Bs in Lisbon and Seville, in preparation for our much anticipated two weeks over there in the Spring. Now, at last, all is in readiness. It is time to put my annual Merry Christmas in writing to you. This is my 40th such note since 1968!

I am enjoying life with you very much in our retirement mode. We have settled down to a comfortable routine. The kids are always a source of joy and worry. It has been and always will be so. That, very simply, is the nature of life when you care deeply about your family. Rather than anguish, it should be a cause for gratitude that we have them in our lives. Your aches and pains are bringing out the best in me, so it seems. You know, everything is a <u>matter of attitude</u>. Increasingly, I am finding myself adopting my Father's (May he rest in peace.) attitude and joy in being helpful. (This could get out of hand.)

It is exciting, at my age, to still have many irons in the fire and to want, more than ever, to make a tiny, but positive, difference every day. As one of my favorite sayings goes: "Some people are sitting in the shade today because someone planted a tree long ago." No good deed is wasted, especially when it is done in response to Jesus' request: "Whatever you do to the least of these, my brethren, you do to me." If only I could do a little more.

Marilyn, I am happy with who and where I am, and you are the one person most responsible for that. My soul mate and conscience. A safe place to discuss problems and frustrations. My moral support. Along with Jesus, the strength which keeps me centered and motivated.

A stress free Christmas and a Healthy New Year.

Love,

Jim

CHRISTMAS 2009

*I couldn't aspire to be a dreamer
without you*

Dear Marilyn Frances,

One of the outstanding aspects of our marriage has been the consistency with which we have gone about seeing the world together. This stationery from the moors and headlands of Mendocino, California is typical of the memories we share. I also include with this letter two other written reminders of romantic and satisfying travel episodes: Wales and Jekyll Island, Georgia. The village of Aberdaron, on the North coast of Wales, seemed to be a vision of the Celtic world of 500 AD, amazingly preserved. Jekyll Island was discovered by us on an impulse, as we were zooming along in the Okefenokee Swamp Country. We both want to recapture the magic of that island.

Maybe Hilton Head, this winter, will awaken that feeling.

Russia, China, Korea, All of Europe and much of Latin America (especially our beloved friend Biel's Brazil) have become a part of who we, as a couple, are. We are, in part, who we are because of the great privilege we have had, and have taken advantage of, to see the people, culture and natural beauty of God's Earth.

For your part in making the Earth my oyster, I am forever grateful. I know you have suffered through some nerve-wracking and physically exhausting exploits which you might not have personally chosen. You lent yourself to my passion. I love you for that. Not that you weren't a veteran of world travel when I met you! But I, sometimes abandoning prudence, have thrust us into a few problematic and hairy situations.

This Christmas I want to acknowledge that I couldn't aspire to be a dreamer without your loving tolerance and active partnership. You have made many of my dreams come true.

My Love,
Jim

Jim McCormick

CHRISTMAS "LETTER" 2010

A bachelor's hubris met its doom

Dear Marilyn,

>One night across a crowded room,
>In a smoke-filled basement of a Church,
>A bachelor's hubris would meet its doom,
>A face, a look would end his search.
>
>And, Marilyn, you still have that look,
>Though forty years and more have passed.
>I'll ne'er regret that vow I took,
>Though forty more years we should last.

Merry Christmas,
Jim

Later Life, and Death, of a Partner
2011–2018

~~~~~~~~

CHRISTMAS 2011

The web of family encircling us with people

Dear Marilyn,

They say that for the young, time passes very slowly, while, for the old, it flies by. Well, here we are at the time of life when the old sphere seems to spin around the sun in a whirl. Where did 2011 go, or, for that matter, 2001, 2, 3, 4, 5, 6, 7, 8, 9 and 10. Why, wasn't it only yesterday that we were anticipating the bicentennial, and the Y2K?

And yet the first decade of the third millennium has brought us, you and me, two precious grandsons and two wonderful daughters by marriage. Much, much has transpired in our family lives. And we are that much richer in our shared loves. The web of family just keeps on encircling us with people to cherish and love.

All of which leads, like a segue, to a realization that our marital love is more than an interaction between two monads. Rather, it is a celebration of a cluster of people whose lives are forever intertwined with ours. And as our love matures and is more spiritual, we more readily take into our circle the whole human race, all precious to the Lord and, therefore, to us. And my love for you will be for all eternity.

Jim

Valentine's Day 2012

Dear Marilyn,
My favorite place in all the world is next to you.

Apparently I am not the only man who craves the feeling of lying in bed very close to the one I love and have chosen to live with.

Your Valentine

~~~~~~~~~~

2/14/12

CHRISTMAS 2012

The anticipation of Ginny and Darric's hospitality tonight

Merry Christmas, My Love,

It is with the shared joy of David and Ji-eun's visit, the anticipation of Ginny and Darric's hospitality tonight (Christmas Eve), the pleasure of watching Cameron and Ben ripping open their gifts, the realization that Dan and Sarah are settling in to a happily married life out in California that we can relax and enjoy life this year to come. While the future is wholly in God's hands and His ways are not our ways, we can be thankful for all the blessings we share this year.

Thank you, Marilyn, for being my partner these last (almost) 45 years! You have supported me in everything I have sought to do. It hasn't always been what you would have chosen to do, but I have always known you were loyal to me. Even when I have been off base, you have been supportive, letting me figure out my mistakes and rectify them. I will try to follow your example this coming year. If so, that will be my gift to you.

Love,
Jim

January 14, 1968-January 14, 2013

45th Anniversary of our engagement

Dear Marilyn,

As they say, "What doesn't kill you makes you stronger." We're still together, and haven't been killed, so we must be very strong! At 45 years we are doing pretty well. I love you still. We two make a pretty good team! Well, a "team of rivals," but that guarantees a good debate. Thank you for being a good sparring partner. 45 years ago tonight you said "yes." (At least you didn't categorically say "Hell No!")

Love,

Jim

~~~~~~~~~~~~~~~~~~~~~

(I was trying to be funny in this anniversary card. There is a lot of truth in humor.)

CHRISTMAS 2013

The kind of love that deepens every year

Dear Marilyn,
With Love to My Wife Today, Tomorrow and Always

As time's gone by, the two of us have <u>shared</u> a lot of things - the comfort and <u>companionship</u> a happy marriage brings, A lot of <u>hopes and dreams fulfilled</u> and <u>memories we hold dear</u> ... *But most of all, the kind of love that deepens every year.*

Today, Tomorrow and Always, I Love You with All My Heart.

Merry Christmas.

Jim

CHRISTMAS 2014

Not an Ozzie and Harriet couple

Dear Marilyn, Honey, Marbabe, Lyn, Sweetheart:
I have been so hard on you, expecting you to be somebody you simply are not. You say I am very critical, and I guess that is true. It must be so. Unfortunately, you are human, with all the baggage that goes with that condition. I am so sorry I try to hold you to such an impossible standard. I don't do that consciously. I guess it is just my personality. As you say, I am tolerant of all kinds of weaknesses in everyone else, but expect you to be perfect. I can't explain it, but I can sort of realize it is so.

You are a wonderful woman. That was surely a big part of my attraction to you back in 1967 when we met. You have a big heart. You are especially spontaneous. You are and always have been my most loyal supporter, by far. I probably have never told you how much that means to me. If anything, you exaggerate my merits when speaking to other people.

You gave me the precious gift of three children to raise together, and you have always been a wise and loving mother to them, being the "principal parent." I have been the beneficiary and, in old age, continue to reap the benefits of fatherhood, thanks to you.

We have never been an "Ozzie and Harriet" couple. That must be nice. We are in sync in every way but our temperaments. That has required work, but we are probably better for it. Looking forward to at least another decade of living with you. Merry Christmas, honey.

Love and a back rub tonight.
Jim

CHRISTMAS 2015

"Absence makes the heart grow fonder"

Hi Honey,

Nothing like absence to make the heart grow fonder! I am reflecting on my earlier single life, and it is so apparent that you are the only girl I ever really desired to live with for the rest of my life. You are that unique friend, soulmate, complement, who never bores me. And with whom I never tire of talking. Cuba has been fascinating. I am too exhausted to write a long letter or to talk right now.

Te amo,
Jim

CHRISTMAS 2016

I want to feel more for you as a fellow wounded warrior

Dear Marilyn,

To begin with, I wish you a Happy Valentine's Day and want you to "be my Valentine."

Someday our three children will probably be going over our papers, reading my Christmas letters and be taken aback to see that there were a few seasons like this one, in which these letters are quite late in coming, signaling that all was not love and kisses on Christmas Day. This year, for example, I had to wait this long to feel inspired to write to you. We just were not hitting it off. Come to think of it, they are observant and mature enough not to be surprised.

Today I can really appreciate your companionship and tiger-like loyalty, your shared values, your shared devotion to our families, your sense of humor, your beauty, etc. But we are, and always have been competitive and argumentative and take offense way too easily, not giving the other much slack. I am critical because I expect so much from you and you can't always deliver. Too bad because we are not that way with the rest of the world. As some wise poet said so well "We always hurt the ones we love." Was it Bobbie Burns?

We see each other as life partners, best friends, sharing everything, so we expect a lot. At least I do. But in reality we expect too much from each other. At least I do. We are (I am) tolerant of everyone's faults but yours. Because I care a lot more about what you do or say.

I live with you, I trust you, I really try to make things easier for you, so any small expression of anger or exasperation coming from you has an exaggerated effect. I am too easily wounded. But more on that later.

This Christmas season was tense. We both were nervous about hosting Biel and his family from Brazil. It turned out that we had nothing to worry about—they are a wonderful bunch of people, but we didn't know what to expect. Biel and Cecilia were here for their honeymoon around 1985, and we didn't know the boys very well. In addition you were experiencing some seasonal mild depression. And as you say, I am becoming grouchy in my old age!

Biel, Cecilia, Mauricio, Bernardo, and their girlfriends couldn't have been better company. Superlatives were in order. And all of our kids & spouses and Cam and Ben pitched in to make it a fabulous week for all of us. You had the burden of seeing that Christmas dinner was fun for everyone, and that went off to perfection. But somehow we ended up in a bit of a funk by New Year's Day and this lasted on and off through January, or so I remember it.

That little book, written by the great Zen master, about learning to practice the art of loving someone, should help us with our personality conflicts, which have existed since we were married, if we read it together, discuss it, and work on his Buddhist insights. As Christians we have the best motivation to "love one another." Jesus, our lord and brother, decreed it as a way of life. But the Eastern religion has much to offer when it comes to <u>carrying out</u> our great commandment. We try but fail, especially with the ones we love the most, to again paraphrase Robert Burns, the great Scottish poet. Love is about giving and not counting the cost, but we are quick to count the cost. We want to put each other ahead of our own interests, but we are quick to take offense. The Zen Master emphasizes compassion. I think you and I agree to that as a key to solving our hyper-sensitivity. Understanding each other's pain and life experiences, and then feeling compassion towards the other, lowering our expectation of perfection as a precondition to love.

Burying the ego is hard for me. I can see that. But it is necessary for me to do that. It isn't about me and my wounded pride. My sensitivity to your small putdowns is a sign of my egocentricity. I need to blow such things off, giving you the benefit of the doubt, recognizing where you may be coming from. I want to understand what makes you tick, so I can feel more for you as a fellow wounded warrior. Life is hard. Full of joy, but also full of disappointments, pain and sorrow. We are no exception.

My pledge today: I will begin anew to (1) burying false pride, try to blow off what might irritate me, (2) work on understanding you more deeply, (3) develop an attitude of compassion towards you, (4) focus not on me but on you in our everyday interactions. In other words, I am going to consciously practice loving you, not expecting anything in return. You already are beautiful, kind, smart, interesting, a good friend and a very loyal wife. What do I have to lose?! A program to work on for whatever time we have together in this unpredictable world. Lastly, I know that, as a woman, words are as important as actions, so I will close with a sincere "I Love You, Honey."

Jim

Story of a Marriage

CHRISTMAS 2017

Short and to the point

Dear Marilyn,

TRANSMITTAL MEMO

READ AND DESTROY	☐	READ AND FILE	☐
READ AND CIRCULATE	☐	SUBMIT COMMENTS	☐
TAKE ACTION ACCORDINGLY	☐	IN TRIPLICATE	☐
CALL WITH ANSWER	☐		

☒ SET THIS ONE ASIDE FROM THE REST AND LET IT REMIND YOU OF SENDER, WHO SELDOM IS WITHOUT YOU ON HIS MIND

Merry Christmas
Love
Jim

50th ANNIVERSARY OF OUR ENGAGEMENT, SHORTLY AFTER CHRISTMAS, 2017

January 14, 1968, our engagement

Dear Marilyn,

Happy 50th anniversary of the night on which we decided to go for broke. In front of the fire in my dismal bachelor pad. How could we know what the next 50 years would bring? We didn't think in those terms, of course. We each knew it was a gamble. We saw failed marriages and unhappy marriages all around us. We knew our church, our guide to Christian life, expected lifelong faithfulness, regardless of how things might turn out. But we each knew there was something special in the other which was worth gambling on. We really liked each other and enjoyed each other's company. We trusted each other to be faithful. We admired each other's values. We had fun together.

I felt something special, unique in my experience. I wanted to be connected to you for the rest of my life. I was aware I might lose you if I didn't act. In other words, I realized I loved you. We have been playing that out ever since, and the future is something to be savored. Let us be real lovers the rest of the way.

Love,
Jim

CHRISTMAS 2018

A bittersweet ode to my dearly departed wife

My dear darling Marilyn,
I am crying out loud in my deepest grief, as I write this annual Christmas love letter to you, a tradition which began the first Christmas of our fifty year marriage. You loved that first letter, Christmas 1968, and begged me to do it every Christmas. I have done that for fifty years. Your heart stopped beating on October 6, 2 ½ months ago. You transitioned to the next stage of our existence. I was left in deepest despair, which has gripped me since that awful day.

Marilyn, my dear wife, your long, slow bodily decline is over. You are in the arms of the Lord. You are at peace. You, I believe, are safely over this fascinating but painful earthly life. I am so happy for you. Your time had come. You weren't going to go on living here forever. No one does.

During those final weeks in the hospital you never really told me how you felt to be getting close to the end. We talked a lot as the situation grew graver, but not really about your feelings concerning that final moment when your heart would give out. For a while we were told you might last up to six months. We were even looking at assisted living for a few days before it became obvious that your heart and your shortness of breath would rule that out.

I was so desperate in my desire to find a way to care for you at home, in our family room, or in assisted living or in a nursing home. Then it became clear one day that you were near death and qualified for hospice. During that whole month I was frantic, going back and forth between our desolate, empty house, where I spent lonely nights, and the hospital, then the rehab center, then the final few days in the hospital.

On the positive side, I lay beside you every day, pouring my heart out with tears, hugging and kissing you as if I could hold on to you and keep the grim reaper away. I must have told you "I love you" hundreds of times, as I continue to do to this day. "I love you; I love you; I love you, Marilyn, my sweetheart, my darling, my baby."

It has been 2 ½ months since you breathed your last, and, when I am alone (most of the time) my mind drifts to images of you all day long and in the middle of the night, and I explode in loud cries: "Oh, honey, I love you so much. I can't stand it." I want so badly to be with you, but I also have the conviction that you are, in fact, with me and our family right now, all the time, just across a thin "veil." Acutely aware, in some dimension we don't understand, of my thoughts and feelings. I really love you, Marilyn, far more intensely than when we were together here on Earth. If only we had the opportunity to relive our long lives together! After my experience of my feelings for you since your passing over, I would love the opportunity to be the loving husband I am today. I am insanely in love with you now. There is nothing like this fulltime mourning to make this surviving spouse want to spend forever in your arms. It is surreal. Maybe heaven will be like that. Not just you and me, but everyone. I feel so passionate about you. I want to throw myself in front of the train to protect you, but I can't. There is no train. There is no _you_, in the flesh.

But we will be together in the afterlife, the eternal life of peace and joy. Right now I can't wait! I know the timing is in God's hands, and I may be chosen to live alone, without you to bounce everything off of, for quite a few years. I guess it doesn't make any difference in the long run. All of us, in our community of loved ones, family and good friends, will experience the joy of one another's company one of these days. It will be such a grand reunion. I picture us running towards each other on a bank of clouds with our arms outstretched and a glorious smile on our faces. What exhilaration! What tears of happiness! What endless joy!

I am so sorry I was not a better husband. I did try. I succeeded in part, but as I reflect on our long, long lives together I see so clearly how I must have disappointed you at times. I guess I was a good husband, maybe even a great husband. I think you would have said so. You told me many, many times how much you loved and cherished me, and that you couldn't have found anyone as right for you as I was. (I knew that God brought us together that fateful night in spring, 1967 in that church basement, at that racial harmony meeting, where your vivacious personality, your enthusiasm for racial justice, your intelligence, your ability to articulate and defend your ideas amazed me, caused my heart to leap, won me over! There really existed such a young woman, who might come to love me as I was already coming to love you. And you were beautiful to boot.)

I am crying uncontrollably as I write these lines. Tears of exquisite joy. I am so happy for what I have had for most of my life. When you said yes my life was set on a new course which would grant me all that I could dream of.

You have been so faithful, so loyal, so militantly supportive of my dreams. Moving up north, running for my dream job as a judge. Really difficult and challenging moves for me, which I would never have undertaken without your confidence in me.

The decision to adopt babies when we didn't get pregnant. We didn't waste time. You were eager to begin the process. Danny came along only two years into our marriage, Ginny two more years. Then a surprise, David. Raising a family, with you in charge, was such fun. What a wonderful family life you gave me. I am so grateful for your mothering, followed by your return to your great gift to the world—teaching. You always made me so proud that I was married to a master teacher who gave so much to her students and to the academic quality of St. Francis High School.

Well, Marilyn my Darling, you who I hope are listening and watching me and these words, I have to go over to Ginny and Darric's house to celebrate Darric's 49th birthday. Thank God for what he and Ginny have created and nurtured, a great home life for our beloved grandchildren Cameron and Benny. As I continue to grieve you, I will sign off for now. You are now so much closer to Jesus, so I will wish you a Merry Christmas in his loving arms. I place my hope in the message of the angels: "Today is born to you a savior, who is Christ the Lord."

And yes, honey, I love you as I have never loved before. I have learned so much about real love in the course of this most painful experience of my life. May I be a better man because of it. I have had to reflect so much more deeply on the importance of really loving. While waiting for that day when we meet again in the heavenly realm, may I love others so much more unselfishly because of my excruciating experience of temporarily losing you, my buddy, my lover, my special partner, my soul mate. Until then, let us communicate with each other all the time, every day, with every heartbeat.

Your Jim

Epilogue #1—2020

Dear Marilyn,

Today is our 52nd anniversary, April 15, 2020. You stopped breathing, and stopped fighting your shortness of breath 1 ½ years ago, but, as far as I am concerned, you are very much my wife today, as ever. I am a "one woman man." Recently, Ella was giving me a pep talk about how I should be open to a new lady as time goes by. I asked her how it is that she hasn't partnered up after Vadim has been gone for a few years. Without hesitation she replied that <u>she</u> is a "one man woman." I had to laugh at the contradiction. I guess she thinks I need a woman in my life because I make such a point of my loneliness. Of course, the point here is that I am lonely for <u>you</u>. No one else could ever fill the place you continue to fill in my world. I have women friends, thanks to you having so many friends, but no one can fill the place you still hold in my heart. Who knows what the future may hold, but I feel your spirit, your soul, your heart, your wisdom, your love as something, somebody very much alive. We don't know enough of the specifics of the afterlife from what has been revealed to know for certain whether you can communicate with me or if I can communicate with you. But, I am operating on the assumption, which seems probable, that some connection, especially a communication of my passionate love for you, can be received by you. And that there is substance to that startling message you conveyed to me as I lay in bed one night two weeks after you died. Out of the blue you "spoke" these words directly to my mind, bypassing human speech: "I will be your guardian angel from now on." I was deeply shaken and, at the same time, thrilled. I really felt I had received a message from you, which I so desperately needed but <u>never expected</u>. Since that night the idea that angels are real, and that they speak to us and watch over us and guide us and love us has been reinforced so many times and in such unlikely ways, from such unlikely people. I was never an "angel" person, now I am, and I have a conviction that you play that role in my life.

I love you so much, honey, and I will continue to talk to you, especially in my head. You may be more real and more accessible to me now than before you entered the spirit world. I am so comforted to be able to talk to you and feel your spiritual (but very real) presence.

Until next time! (tomorrow)

Jim

Epilogue #2–2023

Dear Marilyn,

Two years after you died I suffered a cardiac arrest while alone at home. I called 911 and the EMTs arrived and saved my life. I am sure your prayers made the difference. I am healthy today.

I am celebrating the day you were born into this mixed-up world, November 9, 1941. I had just turned seven. Did I feel you moving down your mother's birth canal? Did I sense you were going to introduce me to the world? You know, you did. You were the missing element necessary for me to be a really successful man. As a judge. As a family man. Without you, I don't want to contemplate what I might have settled for in my life. You have been the indispensable factor. To you, thanks.

Five years after the great trauma of my life I am finally coming back to life and accepting your bodily absence. I know I can carry on. I am confident in your every minute presence, just across the thin line. You and the Lord, always with me. Protecting me. Leading me. Correcting me. You spoke to me after your death. I'll never forget that night. "I'll be your Guardian Angel." Until we are reunited in paradise.

I'm smiling a lot nowadays. All is well. My memories are sweet.

Love, Jim

~~~~~~~~~~~~~~~

(Written in 2023, five years after Marilyn's death.)

About the Author

James McCormick grew up in Detroit, MI, and graduated from the University of Detroit Law School. Shortly after marrying, he and his wife moved to northern Michigan. Seven years and three children later, Jim took a long shot and ran for a judgeship in the Traverse City area. He was elected and served 24 years on the bench.

A lifelong traveler, Jim has explored fifty countries across four continents. He is the author of *Jerusalem and the Holy Land: The First Ecumenical Pilgrim's Guide.*